What they're saying about "Bury Me . . ."

• • •

A neat little book on the commonplace and ordinary that sees right to the core. Nowhere does she preach.
–Kay Urtz, **The Catholic Bulletin**

Each chapter is a complete story. One can open the book at any spot and enjoy a few minutes of her refreshing, often instructive, outlook on life... A bit of Erma Bombeck...a bit of Dolores Curran, she emerges as her own person.
–Ivan Kubista, Editor, **The Courier**, Winona, Minnesota

Provides a gentle confrontation with self...and courage to face the struggle.
–Sandra Graves, PhD, CPGC, Professor, University of Louisville, Director of the American Grief Academy of ACCORD

A winner...one we can all identify with.
–John Sands, Attorney, St. Paul, Minnesota

Full of terrific insights...issues...encouragement.
–Paul Zedek, Director of Religious Education, St. Helen's Vero Beach, Florida

Vignettes of life that arouse so many feelings.
–Jim Zetah, high school counselor, New Ulm Public Schools, New Ulm, Minnesota

Beautiful...affirming...heart warming.
–Marie Wordelman, career lecturer, counselor, Rochester, Minnesota

So much food for thought, I plan to share it with my family and friends.
–Jean Hill, Homemaker, Northglen, Colorado

...it itched the part of my soul that always itches...it felt good.
–Teddie Brown, Owatonna, Minnesota

...global messages in common life events.
–Carol Hoffmann, North Oaks, Minnesota

BURY ME WITH BALLOONS

by Pat Postlewaite

St. Johns

PUBLISHING, INC.

6824 Oaklawn Avenue, Edina, Minnesota 55435

BURY ME WITH BALLOONS

A St. John's Book/ Fall 1991

Previously released under the titles:
Rooted in Gratitude
Copyright © 1987 by Patricia A. Postlewaite
and
·Seasons of the Soul
Copyright © 1988 by Patricia A. Postlewaite

Published by
St. John's Publishing, Inc.,
6824 Oaklawn Avenue, Edina, Minnesota, 55435.

ISBN 0-938577-06-9 (paper bound)

PRINTED AND BOUND IN THE UNITED STATES OF AMERICA
First Edition.
0 9 8 7 6 5 4 3 2 1

To Mom,
to Jim
and to Ann, Phil, and Monica

CONTENTS

B ooks don't happen by themselves, so there are people to thank.

My parents, Vi and Bill Murnane, provided me with a rich and varied childhood that had little to do with money and everything to do with curiosity and wonder. They believed in books, in nature and in me.

My husband Jim, and our children, Ann, Phil and Monica, offered me amazing opportunities to grow and develop. They still do. Much of them is in this book.

Since 1983, when I began writing a monthly contributors' column for the Owatonna People's Press, countless people have said they find my words helpful. Out of that continuous feedback came the courage and energy to write this book.

My efforts have also been encouraged and sustained by Jon Jensen and Bud Phillips of M&M Printing of Owatonna, Myron Eighmy, Dianne Klancher, Barb Nowak and Donna Montgomery.

In addition, friends too numerous or modest to name have been my sounding board, guide and comfort.

CHAPTER ONE

BEST FRIENDS

My mom's best friend died a while ago. Mom had moved across the alley from Peg when they were both fourteen, and they became best friends in a relationship that lasted for sixty-five years.

I was at my mom's when she got the word that Peg had died. I tried to comfort her by holding her, but Mom draws back from being touched when she's hurting. Hugging her then would make her cry, and crying is something she prefers to do in private, if at all.

My mom hates to cry and avoids it if possible. She feels awful when she cries and worse when she's done. What she says works best for her is to get busy doing things.

Crying comes easily for me, both in sadness and in joy. Tears feel good on my cheeks, and I usually don't wipe them away because their wetness confirms my feelings. I feel better after crying.

Getting busy at such a time is hard for me. The activity is distracting and detracting. And so our ways in sorrow differ, my mother's and mine. As a result, we sometimes find it hard to know how to help one another.

After the phone call about Peg's death, Mom said just a few things. She said they had never fought in all those years, not once. Then she corrected herself, "Well, only once. We were disagreeing about something when we were seventeen and I jokingly told Peg, 'Well then kiss my butt'. Peg said, 'Okay I will,' and then I fought to keep her from doing it. For a minute both of us were mad, then we ended up laughing like fools."

Mom's eyes brimmed with tears when she finished, she looked away and started vigorously wiping the kitchen counter, even though it was clean.

When I got home, I sent her a card that said, "Dear Mom, I wish there were a way we could love people and not hurt when we lose them. But since there's not, I'm glad that you loved Peg as long and as well as you have."

Several months later, as Mom and I were dining together, she talked about Peg's last year. It was one of depression, inability to think beyond health worries, and fear of being alone – but dread of living with old people. Mom talked about making hour-long, daily phone calls to Peg, and about finding volunteer work for her addressing letters for the American Cancer Society.

Mom recalled a promise she had made to Peg's husband when he was on his deathbed: a promise to take care of Peg. She had laid awake all night thinking of what that would mean and how she would do it.

Mom said that in addition to never fighting, she and Peg had never caused each other embarrassment nor any negative feelings.

She talked about how they'd laughed together, and then Mom told me something she said she'd never told anyone. For the last year or so, after Peg had moved to a high-rise near her relatives, it was harder for them to get together. The night driving was becoming particularly difficult for Mom.

Mom and Peg soon began watching television together over the phone, for several hours at a time if the programs were good. They especially loved the talk shows, making wild comments about the guests' get ups and laughing like fools at their own comments during the interviews. They tore some folks to shreds for being crass or inane and agreed, with sensitivity, that others were speaking the truth. They watched travel programs and documentaries together over the phone and were touched by many a beautiful concert.

I've often reflected on the things Mom told me about her best friend. I've never had the same best friend since age fourteen. I've never had a friend to whom I haven't caused some embarrassment or pain. I've also never watched television with a friend over the phone. But I'm vastly richer and wiser now because my mother experienced these things and shared them with me.

2

TALENTS ARE SPECIFIC

Although it seems incredible to me, I've been writing a monthly column for our local newspaper for close to eight years.

Back then, Jan Mittlestadt, a "local girl" become editor, wrote an editorial seeking a board of contributors for the paper. This board would consist of volunteer writers willing to contribute on a monthly basis. She intended for the contributions to be editorials on issues that would hopefully create some local debate and result in an increase in letters to the editor.

The idea appealed to me, and I tossed it around in my mind for several weeks. Reading was one of my favorite pastimes. I enjoyed writing letters, and in high school I took a semester of creative writing which consumed me. All these things prompted me to want to say yes.

On the other hand, for much of my life the question, "What will people think?," has lurked in the dark recesses of my mind, jumping out at times to discourage me from trying something new where there is a chance I may not succeed. I told myself that even though my mother liked my letters she really didn't know that much about writing and neither did I.

I put the idea aside until I received a telephone

survey call from the paper a month later. In asking if anything had come of the board of contributors, I was told, "We have thirteen who said they would write. Are you interested?"

I began to sweat and stumble over my words in response. Fortunately the person calling was wonderfully sensitive to my fears and simply said, "Why don't I have the editor call you?" The rest is history.

Response to my work was positive and generous, reinforcing my desire to write. While I knew that my ability was truly a God-given gift, I enjoyed when people commented that I had managed to say what they felt. I won't say I got cocky, but there was a bit of extra pride creeping in.

Then I got a phone call – an amazing, almost exciting phone call. A group of women who liked my writing wanted me to come and speak to them at a monthly meeting! I was flattered. I was tempted to do it. The thought, "Maybe I do have something important to say to others," moved through my brain.

I got more details: where, when, who, how many? Then we talked about topics. The women knew from my column that I had been a social worker for the county in a child protection unit and also at a hospital.

"Many of us are working mothers," she said. "We'd like you to talk about how you successfully manage being a working mother."

It's amazing that such a simple comment could end a speaking career so clearly, but it did. Even though I really wanted to speak to the group, the memory of how chaotic our family life often was prevented me from risking making a fool of myself.

The truth is, for the first fifteen years of my marriage I was a full-time homemaker with occasional short stints working as a dental hygienist plus much volunteer work. Things around the house were chaotic even then. When I returned to college as a full-time student, everyone took on extra duties and kept them when I began working outside the home. It wasn't done smoothly or according to plan. Changes in roles were prompted by survival needs.

The group of women who wanted me to speak were young working mothers who wanted suggestions on how to juggle work needs, family needs and personal needs. They wanted to know what made my life simpler.

I tried to envision myself saying, "Our kids slept in sleeping bags for six years because I knew I wouldn't be consistent about having them make their beds." I could have told them that we had found ways of using a fitted sheet over the mattress and another over the box spring so that it didn't look makeshift, but I doubted that was what they wanted to hear.

I thought about telling them that our kids were allowed to wear whatever they wanted to school, no matter how poor the match, but somehow that didn't sound like what a person does who successfully manages working outside the home. The caller was gracious when I begged off, and I was pleased to give her the names of two women I thought did an excellent job of time management with family and work demands. Then I sat down to examine my experience.

Some people are talented in all aspects of their lives, but most of us aren't. My writing skills are simply that, possibly coupled with a curiosity about life which causes me to be reflective. Being good at this doesn't make me good at other things. At the same time, being less than successful at home-management doesn't take away from my writing skills.

We often have a tendency to expect across the board performance: success in one area should mean success in another. It confuses and disillusions us when psychologists have difficulty relating to one of their own children or when marriage counselors divorce. I was stunned when one of my favorite authors turned out to be an awful speaker.

When we expect people to be equally capable in all areas of their lives, when we lose confidence in them if they don't appear able to do as they say, we diminish them and the good that can come from the gifts they have.

The women who wanted me to speak didn't know me beyond my writing in the paper. I'm grateful I was spared the embarrassment of having them find I had little of use to offer in the area of their interest. I try to keep that in mind when I discover that people I look to for example have unfinished areas in their lives, rough spots that may never smooth out.

We need to celebrate the gifts in one another, to be lavish with words of encouragement and support. We need to be grateful for our own gifts and willing to share them with as many people as we can.

But we also need to be especially gentle with the weaknesses in others. None of us is finished learning and growing yet, unless we choose to be. None of us has it "all together" short of eternity. That's a real relief for me. It helps keep me from thinking I need to hurry up and get perfect, and it lets me say, "No," to doing things that are really beyond my ability at the time.

CHAPTER THREE

No Words
Were Needed

H is name is Paul. I met him one summer in the Pastoral Services Institute at St. Mary's College in Winona. We suffered and rejoiced together for thirteen consecutive days along with thirty-three other first- and second-year master's degree candidates.

As a group, we had class together, studied together, ate and lived together, worried about our papers due in December and wondered if we'd survive. For many of us, our days often ended at midnight and began again by five a.m. We had daily liturgy and prayer services together, planned by the students. We grew close.

It was at one of the prayer services that Paul told his story. Paul is a religious education director. He's also a mime who visits the pediatric ward of his local hospital twice a week. He comes at off-visiting hours, stopping silently to deliver a "Smile, God loves you" balloon to each child. He makes other balloons into animal shapes and does the crazy, happy, silent things that mimes do.

The nurses eventually directed Paul to Becky, a four-year old with leukemia whom Paul was to visit a number of times during her nine months in and out of the hospital. Though they never spoke to one another, each came to love the other. Becky told her parents about Paul and drew pictures of him. Paul talked about Becky with his wife and kids, but had not met Becky's parents.

The visits between Paul and Becky grew longer as their frequency increased. There were always the "Smile, God loves you" balloons; always the animal shapes with other balloons; then more time spent in silence, holding hands, smiling, making faces back and forth, enjoying the sheer delight of being in the graced presence that growing love brings.

On their final visit together, as it became clear to Paul that Becky was going to die soon, he slowly went through their cherished routine and then sat at the side of her bed holding her hand while tears streamed down his face. Becky watched him for a long time. Finally she reached up, touched his tears and said, "Don't cry, God."

Even now, Paul sometimes wonders with regret if he should have spoken to Becky, said something to her in her last hours that she might have cherished.

Those of us who heard the story while sitting clustered on the carpeted sanctuary floor of the chapel during prayer service knew the story was complete. It didn't matter that Becky never heard Paul's voice nor had words of his to hold fast. Becky saw the mime on each of his visits and knew it was God – coming to visit her.

Yes, the story of Paul and Becky was complete even though they exchanged no words. You see, any time we see God in one another the story is complete.

4

THE PATTERN OF OUR LIVES

There's nothing quite so fun as being Irish and listening to another Irishman poke fun at us. I had a chance to enjoy Irish wit and humor at its finest when I attended a weekend retreat given by an Irish priest, Fr. Mike O'Connell.

I knew Mike when he was in high school and enjoyed his wry smile and dry wit even then. He'd gone to the seminary after high school, and I occasionally heard positive things about his work. That retreat weekend, we had a warm and wonderful re-acquainting, celebrating the growth that had taken place in both of us over twenty-four years.

As part of the retreat, Mike talked about his childhood and about a car game the six kids in his family would play while driving through the countryside to visit relatives. It was a game called "Irish farm, German farm." As a farm would come into view, they'd guess, based on the condition of the barn, outbuildings, and farmyard, whether it was an Irish or German farm. Once they guessed, they'd check the name on the mailbox to see if it was Irish or German.

According to Mike, the Irish farms were the ones with the broken down buildings. You're right, that's an Irishman's joke, best told only by the Irish. During these harsh and critical times for the farmer and rural America, no farm jokes are really funny, but Mike was spinning a mood and so it was okay.

He also talked about lying down on the front porch and watching a spider spin a web near the ceiling ("German kids didn't get to gaze at spider webs...their houses were too clean.") The first two connecting points the spider set down were the toughest. Once those foundation points were laid, the rest of the web flowed with relative ease, each intersection in the web adding to its size and flexibility.

Mike talked about the image of the spider web and how it lends itself well as an analogy to our individual lives, which are simply chronological composites of the relationships we've had.

For most of us, the two anchor points on our web were our parents. Some of us were blessed with two strong, viable parents who by their graced efforts started us out with a sturdy, secure foundation for our future relationships. Many of us had somewhat shakier starts, and some had parents that were able to provide only the weakest of attachments, at best.

But just as the spider anchors its web in more than two spots, we too, as we struggle and grow, encounter significant people who allowed us to set down some secure footings as a result of our interactions with them, making up in slight ways for what our parents may have been unable to provide.

Once the rudimentary foundations are laid, each of us fashions a web of intersections representing human relationships, some of greater significance than others. Those major intersections aren't fashioned without risk, effort, or pain. Nor are they able to be looked at without humility, gratitude and joy.

It's common these days for people of all ages to talk about family trees and tracing genealogies. There are a number of standard forms printed for filling out a family tree. Some completed ones look like a birch sapling; others looked like the spreading chestnut tree.

Since the weekend with Father Mike, I've been pondering the relationship web. I wish there was a large standardized form similar to a web on which to jot any and all significant relationships that I've had, regardless of duration, from my earliest memories till present.

On my web, I'd include names of anyone who helped me learn more about myself, the wonder of the world, and the uniqueness of people. I'd highlight those folks who encouraged me, directly or otherwise, to see myself and others with gentle, respectful and loving eyes.

We all have those people of hope in our web, past and present. We also have those intersections which are terribly painful to recall and cause the web to be torn. We're luckier than the humble spider who is compelled to go back and repair each tear in its web in order for the web to regain its full strength.

As we exchange with each other the good news of our present relationships and of God's reality in our life (aren't they the same?), it's possible to let the peace and wisdom gained flow gently back over our webs, healing and mending past traumas in the light of our present understandings.

It's also important to recognize the role we play in helping form the webs of others. Given the choice, I'd like to help build solid intersections of trust, hope and mutual respect that have the power to heal past hurts. I'd like to help build webs that will withstand wind, storm and severe stress; webs that will survive to glisten in the sunlight following a downpour.

Thank heaven that Michael O'Connell's mother wasn't German.

5

IT'S OKAY TO ASK FOR HELP

I'm a believer in professional counseling services for people in emotional pain. I wasn't born that way. The first time I chose counseling, our marriage was painful, and we were stuck in a stage that left both of us hurting for too long.

The realization that it was time for counseling came gradually and made me sick to my stomach. It was one thing to talk with a few trusted friends about what "wasn't working". It was much different admitting we needed professional help. It made our situation sound worse to me, and hopeless. I had a nagging fear the counselor might decide there was something wrong with me, and when he told me what "it" was, I might be shocked, sickened and not able to change. What if I found out "it" was all my fault, or that I was crazy?

It took me three days of not being able to eat more than a bit at a time before I picked up the phone. Then it took four false starts of dialing and hanging up before I let the call go through. When the marriage counselor answered his own phone, I hung up on him. I had braced myself for a secretary, not a counselor, and I couldn't control my fear at hearing him on the line.

As I write this, my stomach churns but there is a smile on my face. While my body recalls the fear of being so vulnerable (and of breaking "family rules" by getting outside help), my memory presents me with five positive experiences I've had in short-term counseling since then. I went twice for marriage counseling and three times for individual guidance during periods in my life when I was in more emotional pain than I wanted to wade through unguided.

What prompted this self disclosure? The night before I wrote this, I got a phone call from a twenty-one-year old friend of our daughter. Both our daughter and her friend are advisers at a nearby college where each is responsible for a floor of girls in the residence halls. Our daughter's friend had heard a grief talk I'd given earlier in the quarter but wanted more information. Grief had suddenly become acutely real to her when a student living on her floor returned from spring break bearing the news of a brother's death by shotgun suicide in the family home.

I tried to be helpful in as many ways as I could and ended up feeling angry and frustrated. No doubt this came from feeling powerless in the face of such pain. But some of my anger also stemmed from the social attitudes and decisions that keep people from healing through professional guidance during marked pain.

How do you tell a college student they will most likely need professional counseling as the result of being a suicide survivor? How do you tell *anyone* that? *Does* anyone tell suicide survivors that?

It's true. Certain losses require the help of a professional simply because the stigmatizing or traumatic circumstances invariably cause high levels of fear, shame, guilt, anger and perplexity.

Most people who have survived the suicide of a loved one or had a loved one murdered need skillful caring from someone trained to listen and provide direction. Rape victims; witnesses to a violent death; people who have caused a death by negligence, or had a loved one die through the negligence of another; and people living with a secret they consider deeply shameful pertaining to sexual abuse or actions occurring in military combat need help from someone trained to see beyond the horror of the moment in a calm, nonjudgmental way. We aren't honest about that. Our social attitude about professional counseling or self-help groups is that they're for the basket cases, crazy people, the weak, or those who can't cope. We've allowed a stigma to be created about those who seek counseling. This has caused many people to put off seeking help for fear it may affect employment or promotion opportunities. Likewise, there are children and adolescents not getting the help they need because their parents fear being labeled failures by a gossiping community.

Is counseling for crazies or failures? Truth is, the healthier a person is when undergoing counseling, the more beneficial the sessions will be. If we could just develop enough trust with one another, the words, "I'd encourage you to get some help for what you're going through," might be heard as a statement of care and compassion, not an accusation of weakness.

I wish we could develop the awareness and commitment to each other that would prevent bureaucracies from pricing counseling beyond the financial means of those who need professional help. I wish we could be insistent enough so that when system after system (school, church, workplace, family) passes the buck saying, "It's not our problem," people who know otherwise would disagree with enough vehemence to see that services are provided to people who need them.

Much healing takes place at kitchen tables, over telephones, and in places where people truly listen to another's pain. But some of life's situations are, by their nature, so brutalizing as to require added help. We need to be honest with one another about that and to assist one another in getting the needed help.

CHAPTER SIX

A LASTING FATHER

My dad died after a two-year battle with cancer that left his bones broken but his spirit intact. His death brought a form of relief to all of us, especially at no longer having to see the tremendous pain he was enduring his last few weeks of life.

The Christmas following his death had its bittersweet moments, the most special being a gift dropped off by a friend who was in a dash to get to relatives. It was a wood-burned plaque still tacky from its final coat of varnish. It read, "I will never forget you my people, I have carved you on the palm of my hand." (Isaiah 49:15).

In my funnier, irreverent moods it occurs to me that the saying makes God sound like He's a hunk of cold granite; something that super-sober Christians sometimes make Him out to be. In my more reflective moods, I know for certain that God is warm and vibrant and so permanently in love with us that He carved our names on the palms of His hands.

Ancient peoples had no other technique for tattooing skin than to carve or puncture the flesh with a sharp object and rub ashes or plant dyes into the wound several times during the healing process.

Unlike today, tattoos were highly permanent and

people gave considerable forethought to tattooing. It wasn't something done as a lark while mildly intoxicated or during a brief infatuation. In ancient times, tattoos were permanent decorations or statements and were customarily on parts of the body other than the hands. A tattoo on the palm of the hand, besides being particularly painful to receive, would have been a constant, highly visible reminder of the bearer's intent.

So it is with God. He is so totally in love with each of us that He has carved our names on His palms as a permanent statement to us and others that He will love us for all time, under all conditions, no matter what we're like. There's no erasing that tattoo, and He knew what that meant when He chose to do it, far better than we.

God's like the stray setter pup that used to always seem to find me on my five mile hikes in the very early mornings on vacation. I couldn't get rid of him. Sometimes it was a real pain because the pup was always so *there*.

But mostly it felt good to have him around, acting the entire time like I was the only thing that mattered in his life. Even when I'd yell at him and stamp my feet for him to go home, wherever that was, he'd just follow at a distance or head off through the woods only to show up a while later. It's not by accident that Francis Thompson called God the Hound of Heaven.

The reality of God's permanent love for me can be a real pain when I'm choosing a course of action that's not consistent with my values. I suppose that's one of the difficulties that comes with believing in right and wrong. But mostly, His presence and gift of persistent, unconditional love means security, joy and peace in my life even if I don't always act like it.

You see, God's not content only to love us no matter what we're like. He's determined we experience the reality of that before we die. Once we have, then it's our decision what we will do in response to that kind of love. After we've experienced it, it's pretty tough not to want to do something about it.

It's nice having a Father like that, and it's nice having the plaque from my friend as a visual reminder of His love.

CHAPTER SEVEN

EXPRESSING EMOTIONS IS A SKILL

I'm still steaming a bit as I write this, pondering why it bothers me when I'm not good at things. I know I'm a perfectionist, in categories of my own choosing, but it frustrates the heck out of me that I allow myself to get mad at me for not doing things right.

Here's what happened. I just defended myself. I spoke my feelings about a situation where I was not being given proper consideration, and I didn't do it very well. I'm new at defending myself in certain areas of my life. *New* translates here into unpracticed, unskilled, in fact, fairly lousy. But regardless of that, I did take a new step, risked something more, and pulled it off, defending myself when previously I would have kept quiet. What bothers me is how displeased I was with not having done better.

So many of us, me included, are infinitely patient with others just beginning. Think about children taking their first steps. They're lousy at it. They lurch, stabilize, sink toward the ground, manage a crouch, pop back up, take a step, and then begin the process again with an occasional plop to their butts. They're clearly learners, just beginning. Yet anyone who sees them is immediately captivated, cheers for them, urges them on, smiles, claps, winks to anyone at how cute and daring the new walkers are, and calls their lousy performance a wonderful job.

We encourage new readers by sitting through sometimes grimly boring books, gently correcting, helping sound out words, chuckling silently at amusing mistakes. We encourage new bike riders by removing training wheels and running like crazy to push and support them on a maiden voyage. We usually laugh at the crashes, soothe the scraped knees, keep running and supporting until we're scarlet in the face, and give dozens of words of encouragement.

Think of the balls we toss, the skates we lace, the tennis rackets we swing, the swimming attempts we watch and cheer, all to give practice and support. We simply expect that beginners will be awkward, unskilled, as adept at goofing as they are at gaining. In fact, we're careful to protect our kids from coaches, lesson givers, and other parents who frustrate too easily and are out for the wins too soon. Somehow we instinctively know the ones who push for perfection too soon can kill the spirit of those starting out to learn a skill.

You know what? Handling anger well is a skill. So is being assertive, expressing needs, expressing affection and becoming independent, regardless of what age we start those things.

I mentally climbed all over myself for not having done a better job of defending myself and expressing anger. Yet last summer I had all kinds of strokes for myself as I learned to slalom ski and cut across the wake. How interesting, and how sad.

Well, I've decided a couple of things are going to change. Being aware of my perfectionism helps. Now that I am, I simply intend to grant myself the same leeway in learning human interaction skills as I grant myself in learning new sports. I expect new sports to take me literally hours and hours of practice before smoothness, if not skill, is achieved. I've decided to expect that the same amount of practice will be needed in order for me to be skilled at expressing certain emotions.

I've chosen a reminder for myself: a T-shirt I call my

"I can do it" shirt. It's a bright red "North Pole '86" shirt, complete with a black dog-drawn sled and the autographs of Minnesotans Ann Bancroft and Paul Schurke. Paul was the co-leader and Ann the only woman on the seven-member polar expedition that reached the North Pole by dogsled in May of 1986. Words cannot express the thrill I experienced meeting them at the State Fair, watching them, talking to them and getting a poster from Ann autographed "chase your dreams."

Well I have a dream. It's to be a healthy, caring woman, interdependent, committed, supportive, who is able to express the full range of human emotions with honesty and regard for myself and others. Those are skills that need to be practiced with the patience and humor of beginning athletes. Those are skills that need time, dedication, and the dogged determination found in polar expeditions.

If Ann Bancroft found the determination for her North Pole '86 dream, I can find the patience and determination for mine. Care to join us?

8

EVIDENCE OF FAMILY

Several years ago we repainted and papered our kitchen and dining room. The two rooms are really one, with the only eating area being in the dining room. I wallpapered the side of the refrigerator to match the walls and make the area appear bigger.

The actual work went quickly; the preparation work was much more involved. Twenty-five pieces of assorted art work had to be removed along with tape that, over the years, had become permanently affixed to the wall.

For eleven years, one of the kitchen walls was our art wall, holding favorite works our three kids had put their hearts into. It seems to me a sacred thing when people put their thoughts and feelings on paper in a way that brings meaning and beauty to others, and I delighted in displaying their efforts at expression.

Once before, I had taken everything down and encased it in a clear adhesive coating to protect it from occasional water fights during dishes, squirt gun fights during warm weather, and splattered batter from beginning cooks who took the electric beaters out of the bowl without turning off the mixer. Seven years later, a fire in our garage that started when our son tried to duplicate a fire safety demonstration he'd seen in school put a grey, greasy film on everything. I was grateful then that the vinyl coating was on the artwork and kept it safe.

A decorator once said that the wall should go for the sake of a more attractive decor. But the wall offered more memories than the decorator, so the art wall stayed and the decorator didn't. Besides, it seemed to me that displaying children's (and adult's) artwork was one concrete way of saying, "I like you. You belong here. It feels good to see evidence of you around the place."

I took the artwork down those several years ago with every intention of putting it back up, even though two of the "artists" had moved on to college. But there was a sudden hospitalization, a health complication, and several months of concern. The painting got hired out halfway through the project. The artwork got lovingly stacked in a spare bedroom, awaiting a sane moment for re-hanging.

The artwork never made it. As much as the kids and their friends had enjoyed seeing the art wall and commenting on it, they asserted their right to recognize a developmental transition. They asked that the artwork remain off the wall in favor of the "cleaner look."

I miss it. It was a visible reminder of who we were and who we were becoming. It personalized our home, told our story. But I've found that another wall has begun to serve the same purpose. This time it's our living room entry wall, and it's gathering more and more photos of us and our extended families. It doesn't have quite the charm and amusement of the original artwork wall, but it does a good job of telling the story of who we are and what we enjoy. It reminds us that we have fun together, belong together, and can count on one another. That's quite a job for a wall...and it works.

CHAPTER NINE

I NEEDED FACTS ABOUT GRIEVING

My parents were fantastic teachers, although neither was trained in that profession. I remember entering adulthood knowing how to do a lot of things and feeling at ease in many different situations. But I didn't know about grief.

My dad died of cancer in October of 1976. Eighteen hours before he died, he turned to me and said, "I guess it's time to call the priest." This was the closest he ever came to discussing death. While he and the priest spent time together in private, I walked to the end of the hospital hallway. I leaned my forehead against a large window and gently began to beat the glass while sobbing quietly. What I wanted to do was scream and wail and smash the glass with my fists. I looked at the churning clouds outside, a picture of power that mocked my powerlessness, and I mentally screamed to the heavens in raw anger, "I want to be God."

As well taught as I'd been about other things, I hadn't the foggiest notion how to grieve. The feeling of losing control scared me. Not only did I fear going to pieces, I also sensed that doing the raging that I needed to do would be seen by others as creating a scene. So I packed in those feelings of rage, powerlessness and pain. Then after a couple hours spent bedside, I went out to lunch ("you need to take a break") with a friend who was eager to try a new restaurant and take my mind off the closeness of Dad's death.

Our family spent the long remaining hours of that day in a true death watch, finally leaving the hospital late at night. Dad died gently, alone, in the early hours of the next morning. No doubt he was granted his wish that we not have to face the pain of being present. We got to the hospital shortly after his death, and all felt relief at seeing his face freed of the horrible pinch of pain.

In many ways his funeral was a celebration, of a life well lived as well as an end of pain. It was also a celebration of an end to the hours of sitting bedside, too many trips to the hospital, and too many high hopes dashed by breaking bones. Carried by that sense of relief and encouraged by "how well" my mother was doing, the following weeks found me denying just how great a personal loss my father's death had been. Over and over I replied to people who said his death was a blessing, "You're right. We'll never have to see him in pain again."

Then one day while searching through the linen closet for something, I found a wedding picture of Dad and me standing arm in arm in church, watching my maid of honor walk down the aisle while we waited our turn. I was clearly both nervous and ecstatic, and he was clearly proud. Looking at that picture I realized that, although I'd never see Dad in pain again, I'd also never see him proud, happy, or playful again. The flood of tears that followed began my grieving and allowed me to feel pain that scared me with its intensity. It made me aware that I didn't know how to grieve.

What do I wish I'd been taught about grief? That it's not an emotion, but a combination of many complex feelings, *all normal*, that nobody wants or chooses. That these feelings of anger, guilt, fear, loneliness, anxiety, helplessness, and despair need to be felt and expressed. Feelings of self-pity, weariness, fatigue, thinking in circles, and not being able to think at all, were mixed with feelings of longing, love and gratitude.

The normal shock and numbness many people feel following a death was not our experience because of the many months we'd had in preparation for Dad's death. I wasn't prepared, however, for the terrible pain I'd feel. I wasn't prepared for the anger, blame, and self-doubt I experienced never having heard Dad say to me, "I love you." Though my life was filled with signs of his love, that lack of the spoken "I love you" was devastating in my grief. I needed to know that this reaction was normal.

I needed to have been taught that it would be normal for me to cry in all the wrong places, such as a crowded church, a crowded grocery store, or at work, where tearful discomfort could cause people to wonder if more time away from the job was needed. I needed to have been taught that tears and seeming out of control would scare others; that people would rush to "comfort me" back into control because they hadn't been taught how to simply listen to grief.

I needed to have been taught that it was normal for my mother to feel terribly guilty about not having insisted Dad see a doctor sooner; that she would also feel extreme anger because Dad hadn't gone to the doctor when he should have and ended up dying just when travel, relaxation and time together was possible.

It would have helped me to know it was normal for all of us to be enraged at some of the tactless, blaming things Dad's friend/physician said in his own agony over Dad's death. And it would have helped me to know it was normal for us to experience selective memory for some time. Mom remembered only the good things about Dad. I remembered only the bad things, or none at all.

It would have helped to know it was normal for Mom to call several times to tell me the same thing, or that it was normal for me to be so preoccupied some days that I'd put the milk carton in the cupboard and the cereal in the refrigerator and cry instead of laugh when I discovered it.

It would have helped to know it was normal that some people would never mention my Dad again for fear it would cause me pain, and that it was normal for me to wonder if Mom really loved my Dad because in her striving to cope, she didn't talk about him either.

Over the years since his death, the good memories about Dad have returned. I'm free now to think about how much he really meant to me without feeling pain. I wish I had known then what I know now about grief. I wish there had been more people able to let me say and do all the "unacceptable" things that grievers sometimes say and do. Mostly I wish I had just been able to talk and cry it out with someone who was comfortable with the strong, conflicting, crazy-like, normal behavior of a grieving person.

There are more of those kind of folks around now, both in my own life, and in general. They listen quietly to the pain of a griever without having to logically argue away the illogic that comes with grieving. I'm grateful for that. It's one of the things confirming my belief that the world is getting better.

CHAPTER TEN

THE
IMPORTANCE
OF OTHERS

Not long ago, I bought myself a gift: two tiny porcelain birds, less than an inch tall, nestled together side by side. We've had some health concerns in our family lately, and those birds remind me of softness, fragility, and the quiet strength that I gain from leaning on others when I hurt.

Coping well is important to me, as is living well. Lately, that has meant turning to others for comfort and support. Some of it is comfort I've asked for, but most of it is comfort that was generously given in so many unique ways by people who cared.

Thinking of how people can comfort one another reminds me of a story I heard about a young boy who was tucked into bed just as a storm was starting. He braved out many minutes of lightning and thunder, but finally called out for his mother to hold him.

His mom held him briefly and then, intending to go back to bed, told her son to lie back on his bed and remember that the arms of God would be around him all night long. The boy thought about that a moment and then reached for her arms again.

"I know, Mom," he said, "but tonight I need a God with skin on."

I need a God with skin on too, not only to calm my

fears, but to make life real. It has taken me a long time to accept God's total love for me, no matter what I'm like; that He called me into being because He loved me even before I was born and made a love commitment to me that will last forever, regardless of what I do about it.

Those truths about God's love for me and all people didn't just plop into my life, they came through other people. They came "with skin on."

I grew up not trusting myself, often doubting my intuitions, motives, sincerity, goodness, and worth. Although I'd been taught that God loved me and saw me as good, deep inside I feared Him and felt unlovable and full of shame.

There's good and bad news in all of that. The bad news was the depth of my self doubt. The good news is that dozens of good, generous people, building on each other's influence, have opened me to the reality of my worth and God's call to live in love.

Among all those folks, I can think of only one who talked specifically and in detail about the Father and His love for me. The others just lived it.

Over time they shared their life stories with me. They overlooked my fears and fumblings, trusted me and looked beneath the surface of my self-deception. They reflected back to me an image of gentleness and depth.

Some of them had to work extremely hard and with continuous patience. The unbelievable thing about this incredible parade of people who have loved me into trusting myself and God is that it continues.

I wish I could introduce you to each and every one of them, the ones I know well and the ones who are in my life only briefly. I know people would say about some of them, "Him? Her? No way!"

God is funny. Overlooking our mistaken insistence that we can "make it on our own," He uses the oddest combination of folks to be "His skin." What I've learned through all of it is that God reaches out to me through you and He reaches out to you through me.

Wow!

CHAPTER ELEVEN

THE WORST THAT COULD HAPPEN

R ollerblades. They look like a ski boot or a hockey skate with a single row of narrow wheels replacing the skate blade. They're used in "hockey country" to allow players to stay in shape and practice during non-ice months. I own a pair. I love them.

The first time I saw a kid on a pair of rollerblades, I couldn't believe my eyes! He was skating up the middle of the street, maneuvering gracefully with a hockey stick, acting as if what he was doing was the most natural thing in the world. I was too far away in a car to see his feet clearly, and I was confident I wasn't seeing things. But I decided to take a better look, because hockey skating on pavement in the middle of July was something I'd never seen before.

I pulled the car up next to him and asked him about his skates. Obviously pleased, he gave me a little demonstration of everything he could do and finished by saying, "They're *GREAT!* You should get a pair."

It took me another month before I was able to justify in my own mind spending money on a pair of glorified rollerskates. After all, I was forty-three, not on a hockey team, and unlikely to find many friends to skate with. On the other hand, I had delighted in rollerskating as a kid, and I was confident this would be quite similar.

When I discovered that my feet were small enough so I could buy a children's size skate (which is cheaper than the adult model, though otherwise identical), the urge became greater. Finally, I reasoned with myself this way: "They're no more expensive than a medium-priced skirt and blouse. No one would think a thing if I came home with a new outfit. But I don't want a new outfit." At the same time, it was too large an investment to make if I would decide they weren't for me after I got them. But I figured I'd be able to sell them fairly easily with so many young hockey players in town. That did it.

The salesman was quite nice not to openly poke fun, although he had a hint of a smirk on his face when I tried on the rollerblades. He made polite conversation, asking me where and how often I was going to use them. But I saw him wink at the new salesman coming on duty while I was shuffling around the store.

When I got home, I headed for the longest street I could find that had no cross-traffic, since I wasn't yet ready to deal with cars. It was shaky at first. The darn things were faster than anything I'd been on before, but oh, the feeling!

I slowed down when I heard bikes approaching from behind. As they passed me, one of the boys who looked to be about ten said to his friend, "Did you see that person on the rollerblades? It was an old lady!"

A couple years have passed, and this summer when I headed out I found myself thinking, "Am I being foolish? Am I really too old for this?" So I applied the acid test for reality while I was skating.

What's the worst thing that could happen? Well, I had pretty well eliminated the risk of cars, so the next worst thing would be a bad fall. I could fall and break my neck, which would kill me or leave me paralyzed. Was that worth the enjoyment I got? But I'd never read of that kind of an injury on rollerblades, so I asked what was the next worst thing. Probably that would be a broken leg or arm. Would that be worth it?

I reasoned this could also happen easily on ice skates, and I still ice-skated occasionally, so the threat of broken bones didn't seem too likely. Well then, what about a sliding fall with a good scrape? Was the fun I was having worth that? I imagined the sore, my clothing sticking to it, maybe a scar or at least an unsightly scab. Could I live with that if it was the worst thing that happened to me if I fell?

I looked at the trees sliding by off to my side and smelled the clover on the boulevard. I felt the sun on my back, the sweat of exertion on my face, and the wind in my hair. I felt the tightening of my muscles, the beat of by heart, the flush on my cheeks and the liberation of moving freely. I decided with delight that the joy I felt was worth the risk.

I still haven't fallen. I still surprise ten-year old boys, and I'm still glad the joys of following my spirit fill me in such exhilarating ways.

12 HIS GRATITUDE WAS UTTER WITNESS

My husband and I had a friend some years ago. He was a hard-driving, fun-loving young man working his way to importance in a major corporation. Driving home from work one day, he struck and killed a young boy who darted out between cars. Our friend had a son the same age.

There were no charges, no findings of negligence. Our friend drank more at parties after the accident and we looked the other way. None of us said anything about the accident to him.

We made a point to talk about a lot of other things with him to keep his mind off what had happened. We never mentioned our deep caring for him or his wife and children. We never touched his pain.

We've known parents whose kids have been picked up for DWIs or for dealing drugs. We've known parents whose newborn has been diagnosed as profoundly retarded and others whose child had a badly disfiguring birth defect. We know marriages that have ended painfully with people estranged from family and faith communities. We know of people whose names have been destroyed because of betrayed confidences. We know of people whose professional judgment has been publicly scrutinized and judged lacking.

While we have seen such pain, we have avoided saying something or doing something because we feared causing more pain or embarrassment. At the same time, we've been just a bit sick inside knowing that somehow our silence might be adding to the pain.

Not long ago I talked to someone in that kind of pain. I'd called to tell him I was thinking of him, fearful he might feel intruded upon or not even accept a call. Instead there was an outpouring of gratitude.

"Pat, thank you for calling. It means so much. You'll never know how the littlest thing, a brief word, a card, a gesture of caring has helped," he said.

He'd seen people visibly struggle with what to do. Others had spoken to him of wanting to do various things but were afraid of embarrassing him. This was not a man riding high on support. This was a man still hurting badly who humbly said he never knew before how much the simplest gestures of caring could mean.

I saw him a couple days later. I hugged both him and his wife, longer than people usually hug in public. No words were spoken. Later he mentioned a card he'd gotten from a casual acquaintance. It said on the front, "I want to help," and inside, "but I don't know what to do." His voice broke at that point, and we stopped talking.

We've all stood helpless in the face of such pain, knowing deep inside that emotional pain like that requires human union of some sort. Somehow we know intuitively that in those times of great personal pain, people need to know they are part of a community that cares – even if it's a community of only three or four.

Pain preoccupies. Mentioning our caring to someone in emotional pain will not remind them of something they're trying to forget. People in that kind of pain can't forget. They go over the issue repeatedly and experience extreme isolation. Their need for human contact is incredible, even while they may seem to be pushing people away in order to be alone.

My friend in pain said it took so little to give comfort: a pat on the arm; an "I care," "We're thinking of you," or "How are you doing?"; a card; a wink across the room; a thumbs up sign. If you'd heard him or seen him, you'd never wonder again whether to speak your caring to someone in pain. His gratitude was utter witness.

13 FORGIVING IS HARD...AND NECESSARY

There was a time when cancer ranked among the things I dreaded most. I recall it being spoken of in hushed tones when I was a child. The feeling in the pit of my stomach when I learned Dad had cancer defies description.

Yet as awful as cancer may be, I've seen it leave a person's spirit remarkably peaceful and whole even while it has wasted their body. I've seen it sap strength from a person's body while that person still managed to mature in relationships, tenderness and hope.

What I've now come to dread more than cancer is hard-heartedness: the bitter, cold refusal to forgive. I've seen that poisonous mindset eat away at a person's spirit and in its most virulent form, spill and spread through generations without relief.

I've seen people keep score of injuries. They count and categorize relived hurts, refusing to express their feelings and get on with life. That very scorekeeping and playing with thoughts of revenge blinds them to beautiful people and beautiful days that pass by as they brood.

Forgiveness. It's a word that can trigger feelings of peace, comfort, relief and joy as well as guilt, shame, discomfort and embarrassment.

There's a quote from Sinclair Lewis that says,

"Everyone thinks that forgiveness is a lovely idea until they have something to forgive." Obviously the forgiver, as well as the one being forgiven, experiences conflicting feelings about the whole process.

A cartoon of two disciples sums up many people's reaction to the need to forgive. As the two disciples are walking together one says to the other, referring to a mandate from Jesus, "Have you forgiven 70x7?" The other responds, "Are you kidding? I'm still working on the first time." Forgiveness is work.

Being willing to forgive means giving up keeping score. An attitude of forgiveness means recognizing that all people make poor choices and mistakes on their journey toward wholeness. Some of those mistakes may hurt us personally, either because we make them ourselves or because we're on the receiving end of them.

"Love Story," the once famous movie of a few years back was known for a line that was utter foolishness:"Love means never having to say you're sorry." The truth is, love means having to say again and again, "Forgive me" or "I'm sorry," because as humans we will fail again and again in our effort to love. Mature asking of forgiveness is not about shame or guilt feelings, it's about admitting that we failed to love.

We must be people who learn to both ask for and grant forgiveness to ourselves and others. I'm not sure if those are skills that we develop as we use them, gifts offered daily by the Father for our use, or both. I do know that to be on the receiving end of gentle forgiveness brings a healing that no chemotherapy could equal. I also know that being able to accept apologies gently and easily brings with it humility and growth.

Forgiveness sounds like a word reserved for the big hurts. It really needn't be all that awesome. Certainly family life, work, or school provide daily chances to be gentle with one another. A quick "I'm sorry" and a simple "It's okay" give good opportunity to practice gentleness. Then if the need to seek or grant forgiveness for a major hurt should occur in our lives, we will have had some practice at it.

It doesn't weaken a parent's authority to apologize to a child, nor does it weaken a teacher's position to apologize to a student. Sincere words of regret weaken no one.

Sad but true, the major hurts we occasionally experience sometime require a sheer act of will simply to be able to ask for or grant forgiveness.

Forgiveness isn't fun or easy, but it's necessary and healing – and it can be done.

CHAPTER FOURTEEN

LIFE TESTS US

Sometimes listening to others who are hurting is difficult because there is so little one can do to ease the pain. When someone shares deep hurt with me, I struggle with the tendency to want to give quick reassurance.

Although I know that just letting someone talk about their pain is self-healing, I want to take charge of things and direct their thoughts to positive outcomes. Such a situation came about when a chance phone call to a casual friend put me right in the middle of his re-opened wounds. We ended up spending a short time together during which I mostly listened.

I went home trying to figure out what I should have said and ended up with memories about things that were said to Jim and me when our first son was born dead towards the end of a complicated pregnancy. We were told, "All things that happen are the will of God, even things we don't understand." Others said, "God tests the hardest those he loves the most." Most said, "There's a reason for everything."

Each of those people thought they had helped us, and went away feeling better about the truth they had shared for our comfort. The memory of how it felt to hear such things keeps me from saying them to people who need comforting. Yet, for all the hurt those statements caused me, the result was positive. It began my life's struggle to fathom God and His relationship to all the hurt in this world.

I have come to understand that God is good, and that only good comes from Him. That which is bad comes from a disordered world, from the free choice of people who can choose wrong, or from natural forces that combine in ways that destroy. God doesn't choose hurricanes, retarded children, starving nations, or premature deaths to test people. God doesn't call people to Himself because He needs them more than we do, as I once heard someone tell a grief-stricken teen-ager at the funeral of her young uncle.

God doesn't test people with cancer, or punish people by inflicting them with AIDS. God is grieved by all those things which bring true sorrow to us. He made us to be happy, peaceful and full of life, and He grieves at anything that takes that away.

In the midst of the pain that comes simply from living as humans in an imperfect world, God is there, not as the source of our pain (as people told me at the loss of our son), but rather as sustenance, comfort, and strength. God is present in the person of others who care, who pitch in and help out, or who sit and listen. But He is there.

God is present in people's gentle humor and words of affection, in a new found inner strength, or in hope; but He is there. His role in tragedy is not as a cause, but as an opportunity to bring wholeness out of the most tragic brokenness.

God doesn't test us, life does. Life tests us, with God close by yearning to help us bring growth and good from the struggles we experience. Growing and maturing means learning to wrestle with setbacks, failure and sometimes tragedy. God isn't there trying to see how much He can load on us before we cave in. He's there ready to coach us to victory, if that's what we want.

CHAPTER FIFTEEN

CUSTOMS CREATE HOPE

It seems that folks either delight in Christmas customs or they don't. I know some who go all out and others who would prefer to jump from early November to mid January in one leap.

Several years ago we were invited to a mid-December chili and carolling party. We gathered as neighbors and friends for snacks and the singing of carols around a piano. Then we headed out to sing carols in the neighborhood. When cold forced us back in, we returned for zesty chili, french bread, and assorted cookies.

It was a new custom for me on this wonderful, late afternoon. But others were talking about previous times, and I was curious. The hostess found an uncluttered corner and told her story over a cup of warm cider.

She and her husband had been transferred with his job at an unexpected and unwanted time. Their boys were in late elementary grades with close friends and grandparents living nearby. But the move was necessary. It came in late November, when people commonly stay inside and neighborhood friendships are harder to establish.

Determined not to have a sad Christmas, especially because travel back home was impossible, my friend and her husband tried to figure out how to fill their home with people and create some Christmas memories from the start. They talked about a variety of plans. They wanted something that would appeal to those who might not know each other well – something that would involve more than the standing around and brief chatting common to open houses.

Recalling that carolling was a favorite childhood memory of many people their age, they stumbled on the idea of a chili and carolling party. It was a hit from the start and filled the house with the sounds of laughter, happiness, and commotion that their boys needed. It was a family party, all ages welcomed, and over the years evolved into one that included infants and grandparents alike. It helped give Christmas a warm glow without being an elaborate affair.

Establishing customs around birthdays and major holidays is important. People gain a sense of permanence and being rooted when customs are repeated each year. Children, especially, find a sense of hope in life from the joy and excitement of seasonal celebrations and customs, and knowing that they will be repeated.

The beauty of customs is that they need not be elaborate or expensive. They need only be consistent and have some special element of joy, peace, or playfulness.

Our family observes customs from when Jim and I were young; we have also developed Christmas customs of our own. Every year when we trim the tree, each of our kids gets an ornament for that year. It becomes theirs and goes into a separate box marked with their name. It's understood that when the kids leave home, they will take their box of ornaments with them so that the Christmas tree, wherever they make their new life, will have familiar decorations that recall happy memories.

We also have unique Christmas Eve dinners. Many years ago we decided the Christmas Eve dinner menu, start to finish, should be selected by the kids. The three of them had to arrive at a mutually agreeable menu, and it couldn't be decided by force or coercion.

Some years the dinners have been short on

vegetables and long on dessert, but for the most part they've been good. Not too many people might have enjoyed the year we started with spinach dip, moved to egg rolls, egg drop soup, rice, and ended with ice cream pie, but we had good laughs and thought it was wonderful. The five of us, plus Grandma, all making egg rolls together in a kitchen designed for two helped make the meal memorable.

Our international phone calls are made on Christmas Eve, and this once found us talking to "family" from Sweden, Venezuela and Sardinia. Other people who also have loved ones far away have told me that they mail a "Twelve Days of Christmas" box, or even a "Month of Giving" box. I saw one such box that had been sent across the United States to grandparents I know. I was fascinated to see the simple but fun gifts, made by the grandchildren, that were taken out and unwrapped each day.

One gift was an assortment of snowflakes cut out of paper to be put on the front window. Another was three reindeer made of candy canes and pipe cleaners. There was a tiny bag of chocolate kisses, an orange studded with cloves, a pine cone dipped in peanut butter and birdseed for outdoors, and a package of festive snack napkins. One day's gift was a tape recording of the grandchildren singing carols, one was poems the family had written.

It didn't take long to realize that a month full of loving and joy had been packed in a box and sent far away. If I had been the giver of that gift, I would have made a calendar for myself and written the description of each gift tucked in the box, with the date that had been put on the wrapping. Each day, as a new gift was being opened, I would have known what it was and been able to share the enjoyment it brought.

The joy of Christmas customs is that they can be so easily individualized. They can be adapted to meet the needs of the family or group who chooses in special ways to say, "I love you," "You matter to me," "I take delight in remembering you." Christmas customs needn't complicate the Christmas season. Rather, they can make it rich and meaningful, simple and festive instead of frantic and commercial. They are intended to be established, cherished, and shared for others to enjoy as hope for years to come.

CHAPTER SIXTEEN

FRAMES THAT DON'T FIT

We have a picture of my grandmother at age eighteen, arrayed in taffeta and ruffles and wearing an enormous hat. It's in an ornate frame that fits the picture. Next to it is a casual shot of our family in a plain frame. Each picture would be out of place in the other's frame.

We all have picture frames through which we view the world, and what we judge to be right depends on our frame. I heard a talk by Sister Clare Fitzgerald of Boston College about four major areas today where people need to ask themselves if the picture frames they look through are right for the reality.

One of these is family. There's no doubt that family life has changed, that divorce and single parenting has changed forever the way families look and function. But the truth is there's no going back. Just as we know it's unlikely our society will return to living in extended families, counseling or wishing and praying otherwise won't change the fact that family styles will be more diverse than in the past.

Our challenge isn't to make it be the way it used to be, weeping and moaning about all the changes in family life. Our challenge is to look long and hard at what was good about two-parent families, what we valued about them, what they did well for children and adults, and then determine how those same valuable aspects can be incorporated into family systems existing today.

That's also true of education. When the "picture frame" of education was teaching the basics, it was relatively simple to provide students with reading, writing, and arithmetic. We're kidding ourselves if we think going back to basics will meet the educational needs of today's youth. Our challenge is not to wring our hands about the fact that it's not the way it used to be. We need to closely examine what the schools did well "back then," decide if those things are still of value now, and then find ways to impart those values in today's schools.

I belong to a church that for centuries has seen itself as an extension of the kingship of Christ. Kings defend their kingship, rule their subjects, make declarations. More recently, my church has come to see itself as a Servant. That's a new way of framing the reality of church. Unless people begin seeing through a common frame, there is little likelihood for mutual comfort. King and Servant don't fit in the same frame. The tasks to carry out the vision are radically different.

Our country has faced a perception shift also. The questioning of the way we previously viewed our country is evidenced by the surge in popularity of Vietnam films. On the other hand, Rambo films are also popular. Our country is run by leaders who operate by looking through two frames at once.

Blind patriotism that once existed in the United States is gone. Civil disobedience is common of people who deeply love this country, and who, at great personal cost, are trying to call it back to forgotten values. Does this mean patriotism has gone or should go? No. Our challenge now is to examine what patriotism is about, what value it has, and how it makes us better people and a better nation. Then we need to bring forward the values of old patriotism we want lived out in this time.

It's never easy to rethink what we've held sacred.

Yet if we don't, our vocabulary: "broken families, inferior schools, vocations crisis, traitor," will betray our thinking. More importantly, the way we act will be determined by frames that no longer fit the reality of today. Anything of value can withstand a probing examination. We must be willing to look below the surface of things we have held sacred to see if they still serve a purpose.

If nothing else, we need to at least be aware of what our frames are. It would allow us to be stronger and gentler, more sensitive and less judgmental with one another. How we frame our reality dictates how we live. That deserves reflection.

CHAPTER SEVENTEEN

HEALING COMES WITH OTHERS

The older I get, the more I recognize how healing comes to us through personal interaction. While I could never exclude the reality of God's part in healing, my experience is that healing comes mostly through others. On one hand, healing is about doctors, nurses, skill, technology, medicine, holistic practices, bedside manner, hope and gratitude.

It's about people sending cards and prayer, telephoning, making meals and listening to fears. It's about people opening their doors for a recuperation or a vacation, or sometimes digging into their pockets to cover bills and needs that would otherwise go unmet. It's about people remembering to visit and encourage.

Healing is about people asking, "How are you doing?," once you're up and around to let you know they're concerned. It's about people welcoming you back to familiar places and maybe overlooking the fact that you're not doing or looking quite as well as before. Physical healing is like that.

The healing of brokenness and inner pain, on the other hand, is about people gradually, and with risk, sharing the pain of their own brokenness. It means sharing their efforts at working toward wholeness and the growth that has resulted.

There are so many things that require healing: disease; injury; rejection; abandonment; memories of abuse; dependencies on chemicals, food and people; and all the things having to do with social, collective, and individual pain.

When people trust others enough to communicate their brokenness, healing can begin to happen. Communicating pain is the beginning of emotional release and the growing self-assurance that comes from recognizing personal patterns, truth, and needs. Those listening to another's pain gain matter for reflection as well as the hope that just as they have been available to someone else in need, so too will there be others available to them in their time of pain.

There is a new mentoring going on today. We are teaching one another about personal pain, the survival and healing of injury from breaking or broken relationships, changing roles, dreams unrealized or never to be, memories of bodily or spiritual abuse, and addictions. In my experience, more people are trusting their stories to one another, individually or collectively. It's resulting in renewed hope, determination, strength, humility, compassion and trust.

I sense a healing going on in others and myself that can only be from God. But it's dependent on true human risk and people sharing their stories with one another. I'm convinced all healing depends on that.

CHAPTER EIGHTEEN

HAPPINESS IS HOMEGROWN

I bought a plaque that says "Happiness is home-grown." Lately I've been thinking about happiness as being inner-created, and "Happiness is home-grown" is a saying that comes closest to making that point.

Through reading and reflection I've become aware of *self-talk* and how deeply it affects the way we feel and act. Obviously, the things we say to ourselves have vital influence on our self-esteem. Many people realize that and are making efforts to change their self-talk from negative to positive.

My husband came home a bit perplexed from visiting his brother Jeff in California. Jeff and Evy had posted small cards with positive statements in the high traffic areas of their home. Now they see and say to themselves positive statements to change their self-talk and improve their self-esteem.

Jim's perplexity over Jeff and Evy's efforts made me realize something else that talking with others has confirmed. Some people are not victims of negative self-talk. Regardless of how it came to be, some people don't deal harshly with themselves. These people often find it hard to understand how enmeshed others can be in defeating, negative self-talk.

Though I wish it were otherwise, I often engage in

negative self-talk. I grew up wanting to please people, almost desperately so. Consequently, I was sensitive to real or imagined rejection by anyone, even people I didn't care for. Over the years I have internalized much of anything negative said to or about me.

When I'm being harsh with myself, I say one or more of the following: "You have absolutely no will power; why do you act so stupid?; you were showing off again, weren't you?; you're a quitter; you don't have what it takes; you never learn, do you?; why don't you work harder?; aren't you ashamed of how fat you've gotten?; you say such dumb things; it has to be perfect or it doesn't count; you're coming on too strong, they won't like you; why do you always think only about yourself?"

Wishing otherwise won't make that kind of self-talk go away, and it obviously serves no good purpose. So I'm trying to train myself to become more aware of what I say to myself and to actively counter with positive statements when I'm aware of being self-critical.

Even better, I'm trying to say positive things to myself from the start. I want to begin my day with thanks and positive statements and say affirming things to myself frequently throughout the day.

There are certain things that help. I may say to myself: "I am lovable and capable; my ideas are useful; I am fun to be with; I am easy to talk to; I have a nice smile; I can help others feel comfortable; I can be open and trusting; I am learning to take better care of myself; God is working in my life," or, "I have all I need to be happy."

We were all intended to love and cherish ourselves so we could, in turn, love and cherish others. That takes high self-esteem. Some people who grew up in solidly nurturing families seem to catch on to the skill of positive self-talk from the start.

Most of us don't have that ability. We need to remind ourselves that for us, positive self-talk may be a skill requiring a lifetime to develop. Positive self-talk and the high esteem that can follow will not result in conceit or too much pride, but rather will result in humility at its finest.

Positive self-talk is a skill that will enrich us so we may allow others to blossom. It's a skill that adds new dimension to the words "Happiness is home-grown."

CHAPTER NINETEEN

LETTING GO OF ANGER AND SADNESS

I 've listened to a lot of sadness and tears over the years, especially since becoming a social worker in 1980. For three years as a child protection worker, I was in daily contact with children and teens who were abused, neglected, and exploited. Their stories were painful.

I also had contact with people who were doing the mistreating, and I often heard their stories. Those stories were painful, too. They made me humbly aware that we know so little of what is inside the people we judge.

Later, when I worked at a hospital, the elderly frequently needed my involvement. In addition to hearing wonderful reminiscences about past days, I heard stories that were painful. Yet as painful and as real as all the stories were, I've come to believe that there is a certain kind of pain many people experience that outweighs all the pains I've heard before. It's the pain of having to face that a parent did not provide the emotional care, nurturing, and support that was needed in a person's childhood.

We all have dreams of an ideal parent, especially an ideal mother. You can't image the pain of hearing an elderly man or woman cry out for their mother to comfort them, especially when they've previously shared that she didn't really provide them with this as a child.

For all the anger and rage I've heard over the years, little has the intensity of rage felt by people allowing themselves to feel the truth that they were emotionally neglected as children. I'm not talking about "bad families" or losers. The stories I've heard and the pain and rage I've witnessed have come from people who grew up in good, successful families where people loved one another.

Their rage commonly manifests in two ways. Sometimes people begin to recognize that they were unnurtured as children but refuse to look closely at the situation because it's so painful. They choose to stuff those uncomfortable feelings and walk around instead as angry, difficult people. They complain in random ways about their parents, get intensely angry quite quickly, avoid intimacy, and may turn to alcohol or other addictions to numb their feelings.

As negative as this sounds, they are often easier to be around than people who are beginning to face a deprived childhood. People who are honestly confronting the emptiness caused by well-meaning but needy parents are in a pain all their own.

It's extremely painful to face the fact one's parents didn't do the job; not just saying it, but experiencing it and knowing it's true. We all hold on to the fantasy of the perfect parent: one who smiles, loves, understands, supports, and delights in us; one who always has time, always can comfort, and always makes the pain go away.

We all dream of the parent who will give us undivided attention, recognize our strengths and gifts, and be proud of our accomplishments. We dream of a parent who shares our values and wants to show us off and be with us.

Few, if any of us, have had such a parent, but the dream is not easy to set aside. And yet, it seems that in order to get beyond being angry, it's necessary to examine the ways our parents may have failed to provide for us. Some people will say, "Don't do that. Count your blessings, look at all your parents did provide for you, and let go of the rest."

I can't give that kind of advice, even though I believe that we do need to come to a stage of letting go. As painful as it is, and has been in my own life, I have to say that in order to get beyond an in-dwelling anger and sadness, it's necessary to internally make peace with one's parent and be done with it. That means walking awhile in sometimes profound anger and sadness at what didn't occur in our lives as children that should have.

For whatever reason, as a child I needed to be included. My mother, on the other hand, needed to protect. It was important to her that my childhood be happy and free from sadness or unnecessary worry. One day during the summer after third grade, while I was playing in the water at our cabin, the daughter of my mother's friend told me that I would have had two more brothers if Mom hadn't had two miscarriages. I was shocked and upset. I knew the girl was lying, and I hated her. Surely my mother would have told me something like that.

I wanted to ask my mom but then I thought, "What if it's true? What if I ask her about those babies and she cries, because surely it will make her sad to remember that?" For several years I kept that secret inside, while growing next to it was the nagging question, "What's wrong with you that your mother won't tell you important things?"

The situation repeated itself a few years later, but this time with an alcoholic uncle. Mom had wanted to spare me from having to know anything about alcoholics. She had wanted my feelings for my uncle to be happy ones, not the confused and painful ones she felt. I was told nothing about the problems of my visiting uncle from California until the day after an evening of his drinking too much. I didn't recognize the extent of his drinking at the time, but I was devastated by his crying at our party.

I'd never seen a grown man cry, and there Lawrence was, sobbing at the end of the evening. He was talking about what a failure he was, how much he disappointed everyone he loved, and how he'd be better off dead. It was awful. I was furious with my parents, my grandma, and my other aunt and uncle for not giving him more support. I went to bed that night frightened and confused, wondering with all the sophistication of a sixth grader whether they would treat me like that some day, too.

The next day I started to yell at my mother for the way everyone had seemed to ignore Lawrence's tears. I was crying and saying how unfair they had been. With difficulty Mom began to tell me what she could about what it means to be alcoholic and that Lawrence's crying wasn't the same as other people's crying. I cried and said, "But why didn't you tell me before?"

I don't remember her answer, but the experience added to an inner voice that said, "You're not okay, because if you were, people would tell you about things like your uncle and your brothers that died before you were born." These things seem almost trivial to me now, except for the memory that they became part of some painful, unfinished business that I needed to work through in my adult years.

Some of the anger people feel about childhood neglect is that somehow their parents just "weren't there" for them. They might have been physically present, home after school with cookies and milk even. But at a different, almost inexpressible level, they weren't there.

Those feelings have the effect of reality, even if other people are certain that it wasn't that way. And the reality needs to be expressed with all the sadness and pain that emerges.

Why would anyone want to go through something like that? Why not just bury those long ago, unmet needs and decide that that was then and this is now? One reason is that letting go of anger means being willing to experience it for what it is – anger at being uncared for when we deserved better.

Another reason is that the recurring anger and sadness keeps us from taking good care of ourselves in the present. If we were uncared for as children, we deserve especially good care from ourselves and those we love today.

But for me, the strongest reason for going through the pain of examining unmet needs as a child has to do with the ability to forgive. It's almost impossible for people to forgive when they are full of anger and pain. Yet before freedom from those feelings can be experienced, it is necessary to be able to honestly say, "My parents did the best they could. It wasn't enough for me. I needed more. But they truly tried, as much as they were able, to provide what I needed."

The reality is that as humans we will all face some day that we have fallen seriously short of someone's needs for us. Maybe it will come as a friend, or maybe as a spouse. For many of us it will come as a parent. If we are able to let go of our anger and sadness at what we didn't receive from our parents, we have a better chance of being able to deal gently with ourselves when we face a situation where we were unable to meet the deep, real needs of someone who depended on us.

It's a painful realization, one that demands our best skills at self-acceptance and self-forgiveness. We deserve to be free of anger and sadness at our parents and at ourselves. That freedom is hard fought but possible.

CHAPTER TWENTY

MEMORIES OF DOING AND BEING

O ne of my strongest childhood memories is of being cozy warm, curled up in bed reading the Bobbsey Twins. Later it was Nancy Drew books, read anyplace I could perch long enough to squeeze in a page or two. My love of words, both written and spoken, remains.

I also remember doing things like cutting and pasting, drawing and painting, collecting, sorting, and saving. I'm grateful that although my parents encouraged me not to needlessly waste supplies, they seemed to feel that money spent to have supplies available was money well spent.

I never remember a time in my life when there wasn't construction paper in the house. Yarn scraps became yarn flowers with the use of a kitchen fork. Pipe cleaners were used for everything. As my sewing and crocheting skills passed my mother's ability to teach and interpret directions, Mom managed to point me to a friend of hers who could take over where she left off.

Our family swam each summer and skated in the winter. I remember early hunting trips when I got to sip coffee with cream and sugar, hot from the thermos.

So my childhood is filled with memories of doing and trying, not in an effort to prove myself, but out of curiosity and a zest for life and learning new things that my parents fostered. I cherish those memories and am grateful I was quietly encouraged to "give it a try."

Memories serve a solid purpose in life. They become even more special as one grows older and more limited in movement and ability.

When my eyesight fails, I want strong, happy memories of beautiful landscapes and flowers, birds, forests, and water. I want memories of seeing friends, children, and the look of discovery that comes from teaching someone something new. I want the memories of books read, things made, and a personalized home.

When my hearing fails, I want memories of music, laughter, and words of love. I want memories of having spoken my deepest fears and my fondest hopes, of having heard the pain and happiness of others. I want memories of compliments given and received, words of encouragement and forgiveness, and words that have challenged my thoughts and soothed my soul.

When my feet no longer take me where I choose to go, I want memories of having been in the midst of issues that affect the quality of life. I want memories of being tired from trying too much rather than too little. I want memories of honoring my commitment to others as well as to myself and choosing priorities that respected my ideals. I want memories of worshipping and serving that bring the quiet assurance of a "cup overflowing."

Those wishes result in a life that looks a bit chaotic. It means not being available to do some things that others find fun or important. Very few television programs can provide me the kind of memories I want to comfort me now or later. Being a spectator for most of life's events is not enough for me.

I'm profoundly grateful for health and vigor that allows me to try new things and repeat old happy ones. I'm especially grateful for "teachers and doers", people who by their words and example offer me new ways of thinking and new challenges to consider. They inspire me to see more, be more, and give more of myself to others.

That's what memories are made of.

21

PATIENCE IS
A CHALLENGE

P atience is a virtue. It's also a pretty odd duck. Being patient with others requires being aware and caring enough to know the situation at hand, when to encourage and prod a bit, and when to wait gently for necessary change to take place.

Marriage can be a real test of patience. Women seem to have a better feel for the pulse of marriage; is it strong and regular, or weak and halting? Some of us approach a less than ideal marriage like we'd approach a huge household task. We want to roll up our sleeves and get things done immediately. That's great for garages and kitchen floors, but it can be deadly for marriage relationships.

Being a parent of a child is also a testing ground for patience. What seems so clear to us from the wisdom of our life experience often isn't so clear to our offspring. Knowing when to react or intervene and when to stay supportively in the wings is a real challenge.

The growing-into-independence behavior of teens can give the best of us fits. Patience may be our sole salvation as we live through challenges to our thinking, values, comments about our behavior and appearance, testing of all the rules, voracious appetites, and mood swings. Obviously, reacting with guns "loaded for bear" results in much unnecessary noise, wasted ammunition, and likely damage, especially if the matter mostly needs patience.

For many perfectionists, being patient with themselves is a challenge. I've tried a number of approaches to gain patience with myself and find that frequent reminders help. This saying by Ralph Waldo Emerson is near my bed:

> *Finish each day and be done with it...You*
> *have done what you could; some blunders*
> *and absurdities no doubt crept in; forget them*
> *as soon as you can. Tomorrow is a new day;*
> *you shall begin it well and serenely.*

The greatest challenge to patience can frequently be found in churches, where groups of people need to resolve their differences, face their fears, surrender their false securities and employ trust in the process of moving forward with legitimate and necessary change. At those times, patience with others is essential.

Sometimes resignation or doing nothing may look like patience, feel like patience, or be pawned off as patience. It's really the abdication of responsibility. Problems don't solve themselves, and waiting patiently for something to happen may result in a much worse problem down the line.

In all aspects of life, ignoring a matter may be wrong. So being patient doesn't mean looking the other way. If we've examined every option we could think of and planted some seeds of solution, then patience is proper. On the other hand, if a bona fide problem exists, action needs to be taken. That's when it's time to pray for wisdom and courage, and patience to develop them.

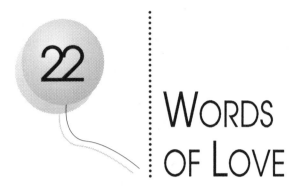

CHAPTER TWENTY TWO

WORDS OF LOVE

I t seems to me that women can speak the language of love.

Maybe this is culturally induced or comes with our ability to mother. Wherever it comes from, being able to speak the language of love is precious and should be celebrated. Beyond that, it's a skill worth teaching or trying to imitate. As risky as it is, it's worth watching, trying a little, and then doing.

I'm all for talking about hockey, IRAs, winter vacations, the gymnastics team, new recipes, and old cars. Those things are fun. But as I move through life, I also need to hear about how other people experience and cope with living. Those are love words.

To share with another the pain, anger and frustration felt toward a parent who is not coping with a spouse's death is a gift of trust in our mutual journey as humans. That kind of sharing is precious and calls for respect. To share the pain of a depression, the fear of "losing it" and the help one received; those are words of love.

To share one's joy at the meaning of life, to speak of things that enrich and stir one's soul and bring renewed hope; those are love words. They are words that confirm our own unique experience of humanity, offered to someone else out of a need to be expressed or for the benefit they may bring.

The most direct of love words, though, are words of appreciation, like: "Thank you; you mean a lot to me; your sharing helped me; your friendship is so important to me; I love your sense of humor; I appreciate your concern for others; I enjoy our conversations; thanks for working so hard; your openness helps me; I tried what you suggested and it worked." These words of direct, loving feedback are essential.

Love words are risk words. The speaker risks standing exposed while the receiver decides how to react. The risk of being misunderstood or rejected is inherent in each statement of love. But so is the chance of connecting, supporting and building mutuality – the right to be listened to and cared about.

It seems that most women are better at love words, that such a vocabulary comes easier for them. But even for some women, family customs or childhood experiences have made them as awkward at love words as many men.

What does our culture hold out as an ideal for most men these days? The Marlboro man is the standard: cool, control, on top of the situation, singular, separate, no vulnerability, directing life.

God love the men who suffer enough pain from that kind of sham to turn their backs on it and risk being vulnerable, real, and appreciative. I love them. They're out there. There are men, risking and fearful, who are learning to touch and embrace tenderly and supportively. They're learning to do that with each other as well as with women. There are men who are learning to speak of their weakness and fears, and revealing how important others are to them.

Some of the most tender words I've heard a man utter were part of a huge bear hug given my husband by a friend who has since died. At the time, George was robust and tanned and in love with life. As we got ready to leave him, he threw his arms around Jim and said,

"Postie, you're just like a brother to me." My eyes brimmed then and now.

We can all learn to connect. We can all learn to speak words of love. And for those of us who are already able to, it's vitally important that we do so.

As people learn to open up, things don't always go well. Some people starting to risk begin with little confidence and fragile self esteem. Those people need our love words. They need our reflection of the good we see in them to help buffer the rejection they may experience from other people as they learn to speak love more easily.

Whether we are men or women, life lived the "Marlboro way" means somebody wins and somebody loses. When life is lived with love words spoken, nobody loses.

CHAPTER TWENTY THREE

KNEE-SLAPPERS

Sometimes memories of my grandparents flood my mind, bringing smiles and frequent laughter. I remember them as being very devoted to one another, hard-working, practical and fun-loving. They're the only people I ever remember who talked about knee-slappers. How I came to love that expression! My first knowledge of a knee-slapper came many years ago when Gramp was showing a family gathering how he got Nanie into her corset after her arthritis made that a two-man job.

Gramp lifted his leg in the air, grimaced to show supreme effort, and demonstrated how he crammed Nanie into her corset with the use of one leg, two hands, and the wall for support. When Gramp finished his tale, complete with groans and spasms, he and Nanie looked at each other and laughed till tears ran down their cheeks. All the while they laughed they slapped their knees. Nanie finally ended it by saying, "Now that's a real knee-slapper."

She had her own knee-slapper story to tell. Nanie detested Gramp's limburger cheese and was also irritated that at the young age of seventy-eight he'd begun napping after their big meal at noon. One day, in retaliation for his sleeping overly long, Nanie smeared a thin film of the cheese on Gramp's upper lip as he slept. When he awakened, she dutifully and solemnly followed him around the house helping him track down the origin of the detestable stench of which he was aware.

They checked dish rags, wastebaskets, and the vegetable cellar. Gramp was beginning to suspect the rotting carcass of a dead mouse between the walls when he spotted shininess on his upper lip while passing a bedroom mirror. By then Nanie was leaning against the doorjamb in the beginning throes of a real knee-slapper.

My grandparents were deeply spiritual people. They prayed together frequently during the day and sang hymns together sitting on a couch in the front room. Both had beautiful voices they loved to blend in praise of God. They also had a gift for somehow combining their humor and deep spirituality in ways that were delightful. They had a healthy, playful, holy irreverence. The memory of that humor made Nanie's final knee-slapper a true family story.

My grandparents came to live with us for awhile because of some extenuating circumstances. Not long after, they needed nursing home care. They would sit together in their room and sing the songs they loved, but Nanie missed being able to toss her one leg over Gramp's lap the way she used to do on their own couch at home.

When Nanie died, Gramp wanted her favorite hymn sung at her funeral. But his hymn books were in another town, locked in their empty home, and our church used different songs. We called ahead to the town where the funeral would be, and the song was not known there either. So we searched around and found the song a matter of hours before all of us needed to leave for the three-hour trip to the service.

Gramp decided the matter was simple. "Patty, you sing the song and then when you get to the funeral home you pull Frank aside and practice it together. He has a beautiful voice and the two of you will do fine."

I'm not a singer, but my grandma was special to me. So I practiced the hymn in the car and arrived in Paynesville relatively calm. I searched out Frank after visiting with the relatives and told him of Gramp's request.

"Patty," he said, "I don't read notes! You'll have to teach it to me."

We dashed down to the basement of the funeral home to practice in earnest. I began to sweat and make mistakes. After awhile it came a bit easier, but we were still far short of funeral singing quality. So I tracked down Gramp and told him our dilemma.

"You'll do just fine," he said. "The Lord will help you."

Frankly, I couldn't figure out how to dispute that, so we just kept practicing. Frank and I were to sing from the rear of the funeral home. Gramp and our immediate families were at the front, close to the casket, so I wasn't petrified, just terribly nervous. To calm myself, I kept thinking about Nanie's love for her hymns. She would have found this particular situation quite amusing.

Our three children were young then, two at the age where they wanted to be sitting on laps. With me not available, Jim had found a close friend to hold our youngest daughter.

The funeral-home service was personal and lovely, and by the time Frank and I sang, I was moved to be able to be a part of it. Unfortunately, it didn't go well. Frank's voice was lovely and full, but he forgot the melody! My voice was barely adequate and couldn't provide the stable direction he might have been able to follow. As his voice wandered from the melody, mine followed, but we persisted.

When we finished, beyond earshot of us but in a strong whisper that was heard by most of the people in front, our daughter Monica looked proudly and wistfully into the face of the person who held her and said with love, "They sound just like the dog on Sesame Street."

Now that's a real knee-slapper!

CHAPTER TWENTY FOUR

BURY ME
WITH BALLOONS

I hope they bury me with balloons. I'm not sure if the balloons should be in a dignified clump where the casket spray usually is, or if they should be flying high on a flower stand. Actually, I'd prefer a huge bank of them; a streamer of dozens of balloons tied together, like I saw when the Minnesota Twins won the World Series.

I want lots of helium-filled balloons at the gravesite. After the final blessing, I'd like anyone who wants a balloon to take one. I'd like a message of joy tied to each balloon, so that people who took one would have an additional moment of happiness.

I know that sounds like "sweetness and light", but when I'm really honest with myself, when I'm fairly centered and can set aside the rushing around that too frequently consumes me, I'm forced to admit that life has been incredibly wonderful. In spite of setbacks, disappointments and pain, I can settle down and reflect on the fullness of my life: the surprises, delights, quiet joys, and lasting peace. It doesn't take long to realize that my life has been a true adventure that I probably wouldn't have the courage to do again. It somehow needs balloons to mark its ending.

I started thinking this way several years ago when five people in my family died within six months. Three of the deaths were totally unexpected: a plane crash, a heart attack, a ruptured aorta. All those people were "too young to die", and we ended up planning funerals with little feel for what kind of service the people now dead would have wanted.

For a while after those funerals, I thought about death a lot. I remembered a few years before when I had knelt in a ditch and prayed over a woman I'd met an hour earlier. We'd shared a meal together with a group of people. She sat across from me, talking and laughing in an easy banter unique to her. She was killed instantly in a car crash, and I got there just after it happened.

There I was, kneeling and holding the hand of a woman who had been full of life not more than ten minutes before. I had always thought in the back of my mind that I would die of cancer, that I would have time to gradually let go of life. I remember thinking that there were things unsaid in my life, important, loving things that were waiting for "the right time." I resolved then to start telling people how much they meant to me, even at the risk of being thought strange.

After that experience I began thinking and planning funerals for my husband, our three kids, and myself. It seems funny when I think of it now, but at the time I was totally immersed in the reality of death. It had so suddenly intruded upon my life.

I shed some tears, wrote some plans, and thought about how I wanted to be remembered. I talked with Jim and the kids about my plans and asked them what kind of funeral they would want if they should die suddenly. Surprisingly, it wasn't morbid or scary for them. In fact, our kids even ended up talking about what they'd like done with the treasures they had at that time: stereos, stuffed animals, beer can collections, favorite books.

I remembered my dad's funeral and how special it had been to tuck goodbye letters and school pictures into his casket. I remembered being alone with my grandma when she died and realizing that next to birth, death was the most profoundly moving experience I had witnessed.

I even ended up devoting one of my monthly newspaper columns to thoughts about death, funerals, and balloons. It was that very column that ended up bringing me face to face with the kind of surprise that will demand balloons as a statement of my life when its ended.

I'd been at work, putting in extra time because of a large number of elderly people in the hospital. I was behind schedule, low on groceries, needing to do laundry, preoccupied, and tired. I rushed into the house intending to get things into shape immediately and was stopped short by the most enormous bunch of balloons I'd ever seen outside a circus.

There in my living room was a collection of helium filled, mylar balloons surrounding a huge, red heart. There were so many, I forgot to count; so many that a year later when we took them to the airport to greet our daughter back from Venezuela, we were mistaken for balloon vendors! The attached card, from a friend who has known the agony and the ecstasy of life, said simply, "Enjoy them now."

For a long while, the generous gift of balloons and the message on the card reminded me only that I had a playful, loving friend who had enjoyed my column and wanted to show her affection. Yet with time, I came to appreciate that "Enjoy them now" was the very focus I wanted my life to have. I wanted to regularly recognize and enjoy the richness of life, loving and being loved, and being part of an unending human adventure that deserves to be recognized and celebrated.

And so I hope they bury me with balloons. Because as far back as I can remember, balloons have represented the ultimate in celebration. When it's done, I hope my life will, too.

CHAPTER TWENTY FIVE

LASTING WOUNDS CAN SERVE OTHERS

F r. Jim Young was keynote speaker at a weekend conference for separated, divorced and re-married Catholics. It was a workshop that seemed to be essential to me as a part-time parish worker. His words had a lasting impact.

At one point, Fr. Young read an account from the Gospel of John about the time Thomas the apostle was in the upper room with the other apostles, having refused earlier to believe that Jesus had appeared to them after the crucifixion.

Thomas, who gave birth to the term "doubting Thomas", had refused to believe his friends' account of Jesus' presence, stating emphatically that until he could personally probe the wounds of the crucifixion, the nail holes and the pierced side of Jesus, he would not believe in Jesus' return from the dead.

When Jesus appeared again, Thomas was present. Jesus called Thomas over and invited him to probe the wounds and see for himself that the testimony of the others was true. While Thomas' earlier disbelief had not been totally out of line with the Jewish belief in spirits and ghosts, the account says that Jesus praised those who believe without having seen.

The sermons preached in church after this reading

usually focus on how frequently we doubt, and how easily our trust is shaken. So I settled down expecting Fr. Young's talk to develop along those same lines.

What I heard was this: possibly we miss the boat when we concentrate on Thomas' disbelief and thereby miss one of the key parts of the story. *Jesus had wounds after the Resurrection.* Maybe we need to reflect on what that means for those of us who are wounded, especially because most Christians believe that Jesus' body was in its perfected state after the Resurrection.

Could it be that life's wounding will be the same for us? Will some wounding be so deep that it lasts forever? Many popular self-help books seem to encourage us to hurry up and get better. How does that fit with the image of permanent wounds? Can it be that those permanent wounds will become permanent scars, present but not in danger of destroying us?

Since then, I've thought a lot about Jesus meeting Thomas' need for proof by offering His wounds to be probed. To me that's one of the most positive things about wounds or scars. At a certain point in recovery, some people are able to show their wounds to others and display the scars of their own life experience. These scars can then be probed and examined by those who need the help or reassurance that comes from knowing others have suffered and survived.

None of us can come through life without scars. Some of us have scars of tremendous proportion from divorce, abandonment, abuse, suicide, the death of a child, or other events that crush out hopes and dreams for the future and change life forever. Yet I've personally known people who have survived deep trauma in each of those situations. They are courageous, caring people who, once they have mended some, have offered their story as a gift to others with knowledge of its power to strengthen and heal.

Wouldn't it be awful if the sufferings we face and the traumas we experience couldn't be shared? Thank God we can support one another in times of great pain.

But even more importantly, thank heaven that people who have been wounded somehow find courage to share their experience and methods of survival with others.

Hope is born, for many of us, in listening to the stories of survivors. Hopefully, we can all learn to humbly share the wounds we've survived in order that others might trust that life can transcend the injuries of the present.

CHAPTER TWENTY SIX

An Awe of
the World

My dad would probably have been called a Renaissance man. If not that, he at least deserves to be know as someone who marvelled at everything having to do with nature.

I don't remember that he was particularly interested in how people thought or in what made them tick, but his interest in nature and his love of all it offered are my strongest childhood memories.

Coming home one day from a country church near a cabin we rented, Dad stopped the car, rolled up his Sunday suit pants, and waded into a marshy ditch. He went well deeper than his pants would allow, saturating them in what we considered to be stinky water. All the while my mom kept calling out the window, "Bill, what are you doing? What are you after?"

He had taken an empty thermos with him, so we felt certain whatever he was after wouldn't be huge. But he roamed around in that ditch far longer than interested my brother and me. We were only mildly curious by the time he returned exclaiming, "I've got hylas."

As we drove back to the cabin he described "hylas" as small frogs that swallow air and puff up sacks below their mouths to enormous proportions. It was hard not to get excited by something that sounded so unique, especially with Dad so obviously pleased.

Birds were his love. He knew hundreds by sight. He knew their migratory patterns, mating habits, and nesting styles and could imitate their calls. As a child I was thrilled when he would coax the female goldfinch into answering him, thereby leading us to her nest. Each winter he'd be pleased when the colorful Canadian birds gathered at his winter feeders on the edge of the woods in plain sight of the cabin.

He marveled with me at salamanders, snakes and lizards. It didn't occur to me to be frightened of them or think they were gross because he was so fascinated and pointed out such interesting facts.

We seldom missed an eclipse of the sun. Long before I understood what they were or why we held two negatives together to watch through, I sensed Dad felt there was something sacred in all of it.

We used to make fun of him because of his interest in cameras, groaning about having our pictures taken, or flatly refusing. Now I feel sad that we didn't appreciate his love for photography. But as much as we poked fun at that, I don't remember ever downgrading his love for nature.

Dad had a small telescope. He would mount it on a camera tripod to stabilize it while we looked at the moon from a bank at the cabin. We had to wait until close to eleven at night for the moon to clear the pine trees, but if we wanted, he'd wake us up, spray us with insecticide, and take us out to sight the telescope and have a look.

Though he could afford it, he waited years to buy himself a better telescope. I was in high school when he finally did, though I remember him looking at them in catalogs for what seemed like years before. He was thrilled with the new telescope and sent away for maps to help us locate craters of the moon.

By then we no longer had trouble staying up until eleven, and Dad would perk a pot of coffee and put it on a stool next to the scope. The nights were still and very black. Sometimes a loon would call, and we'd abandon the scope to watch in silence as it drifted into the light of the moon against the lake.

He knew so much, and sometimes it bothers me that all that knowledge died with him. I remember a fair amount, but I can't identify varieties of pine trees and hardwoods or remember their needle patterns or leaf structures.

I can recognize agates and quartz and a few other rocks he'd tell about as we went agate hunting, but for the most part that knowledge has left me.

Dwelling on what ended with him is sad, and it's only part of the story. Without preaching, forcing or commanding, Dad passed on to those around him an awe of the world and a sense of its beauty. He knew that the earth was saturated with goodness and beauty, and he taught us by example to soak it up.

CHAPTER TWENTY SEVEN

THE MIRACLE
OF CHRISTMAS

W e put up our Christmas tree and decorated the living room on a Sunday that was surprisingly calm. Amidst the unwrapping of stored Christmas treasures and ornaments from years past, our youngest was leisurely wrapping presents at the dining room table, answering the telephone, and making comments to us in the living room.

Our oldest did a bit of decorating, helped with the launching of the tree, and talked about college and new events in her life. She organized the decorations and tended the fire.

Our middle child was still at college. But he became a part of the group in our talk and laughter about the year his close friend worked at stretching a squirrel skin onto a taxidermy mount while Phil called instructions from his place at the tree.

Jim read the paper, planned the display of outside lights, and got ready for his specialty: the art of hanging tinsel on our short-needled pine. His patience with tinsel is beyond what any of us can match. He methodically places each silvery piece, strand by strand, until the tree radiates.

Boyfriends stopped by. There were short breaks for food and the finding of a video for later in the day.

As I moved around, placing things brimming with memories, chatting easily with those I love, dancing a bit to relatively tolerable music, I relished the richness of the day. It occurred to me that there's a wonder about the Christmas season that's unlike any other wonder. Thinking about this Christmas wonder triggered thoughts of the early stages of our marriage.

By our second Christmas, we were soon-to-be parents, our baby due in late January. It was an exciting time when toys, babies and Christmas took on a special significance. We talked and dreamed about the following Christmas when we would have a toddler to delight in.

Yet through the joy of it all, I would sometimes lie awake at night and wonder what having a baby was going to mean. I knew the love Jim and I had for each other, but I wasn't sure what it would be like with three of us. Although I couldn't say it out loud, the nagging question was, "Will there be enough love for all of us?"

Then Ann was born. She was an energetic, captivating child, and I learned quickly that there was enough love for her in our family. Shortly after, I was pregnant again. The question about enough love returned but remained untested. Our first son died prematurely, before delivery.

Even so, three wonderful Christmases passed, filled with building blocks, rocking chairs, bouncing horses, baby dolls and family celebrations. Then we were pregnant again, hopeful and fearful after our failed pregnancy, eager for another child, yet cautious with our feelings.

My silent, middle-of-the-night questions returned. "How can we possibly love another child the way we do our first? Will there be enough love this time so that everyone can get as much as they need and still have enough to share?" This time the questions were stronger, the fears were greater. Yet with the birth of our son, Philip, the answer was still just as clear.

The question repeated itself throughout my pregnancy with Monica, and again from time to time as close friendships expanded to include others. Ever so slowly, I learned through experience that with love, the answer to, "Will there be enough?," is always, "Yes!"

That's what I sensed while decorating and remembering. That was what filled me with quiet joy as I looked at my family and knew that the years to come would expand its size with more and more people.

That's the message of Christmas, made real by the birth of the Christ Child. God had love enough and He poured it forth, gifting us with His only son. He assured us, in doing so, that if love is real, there will always be enough of it to include one more in its embrace.

It's the knowledge of "love enough" that prompts Christmas generosity, cheer, and celebration. The miracle of Christmas, of love born among us, is that love reaches out and is given to us to give to one another – again and again.

CHAPTER TWENTY EIGHT

OLD WOMAN IN THE SNOW

She was slumped in the snow, huddled in a driveway when I first saw her. I was driving down a side street after a moderate snow, only half paying attention, engrossed in thought about an earlier conversation when I realized an old woman was sitting in the snow.

It frightened me to see her. She wasn't crying out. She wasn't panicky. But she was clearly sitting alone at the entrance of the driveway in weather that must have quickly chilled her to the bone, sitting as she was on snow the plow had left piled behind.

I pulled the car in front of her, stopping on the wrong side of the street. "Are you hurt?" I asked.

"No," she said quietly, "but I've fallen and I can't get up."

As I braced myself and extended an arm for her to grab hold and help pull herself up, I noticed frosted moisture on the hairs of her face. She had been here awhile, and yet she appeared calm as she explained about losing her balance while walking in the piled snow of the driveway.

"I thought I could get across it without going into the street, but I lost my balance and sat down instead of falling." She straightened her coat, adjusted her scarf and started to slowly shuffle away from me.

"Where do you live?" I asked, and only vaguely understood since she pointed down the side street to houses I knew belonged to someone else. "Let me take you home," I said, truly concerned. She appeared to be in her eighties, not frail, but certainly not able to manage more than a shuffle in the snowy streets.

"No," she said, "I'll be just fine. I came outside because I need to get some exercise." And with that she thanked me and shuffled off.

I turned the car around and sat watching her shuffle. Then my concern for her took over, and I decided that she shouldn't be allowed to continue on her own. Pulling the car up near her and rolling down the window, I intended to insist that she accept my offer of a ride or vow to follow her slowly until she was safely home. It never happened.

Instead, I watched a proud, determined woman shuffle as best she could, swinging her arms briskly to get more exercise and probably warm herself more quickly after the time in the snow.

Somehow, the risk of hurting her self-pride bothered me more than the thought of her falling again. And yet that didn't seem right either. "Why aren't these decisions easier to make," I thought. "What's the right thing to do? What if she falls? What if she has Alzheimer's and ends up wandering for blocks on end?"

Then I recalled her quiet manner, her calm voice as she told me of losing balance. I remembered her apparent absence of fear as she sat in the snow, watching confidently for a car that would stop or a person that would come to her aid. I admired her.

The busyness of the Christmas season dimmed the memory of that day until I read the following:

> *"Courage does not mean the elimination of fear. Courage means acting in spite of the fact that we are afraid."*

I knew in my heart that the old woman in the snow

had been courageous. She was afraid from her fall; afraid of a harder fall and what it would mean in darkness or on a less-travelled street. Yet she was determined not to let the fear she felt further restrict her already restricted life.

I knew she had shuffled off at a snail's pace fearful that she might fall again, yet with a courage that drove her to act in spite of this. She was still walking, after all. She was still her own boss and able to convince someone else to let her try it on her own.

Someday, someone will no doubt decide the risks of harm to her are too great for her to be allowed to manage on her own. I'm glad I got to meet her before that time. Sitting huddled in the driveway, she gave me a lesson in courage I might never have known.

CHAPTER TWENTY NINE

I HAVE
A FRIEND...

I have a friend who believes in me. We don't see a lot of each other because often times we're too busy, and other times we're too busy thinking we're too busy, and other times we just don't get together because that's the way we are.

More often, we talk on the phone. But even then it's usually with a purpose. The only time we talk just to shoot the breeze is on the tail-end of a crisis, when we've talked for several days in a row in a hard, necessary-to-survival kind of talk.

The kind of things she says to me are, "No, you're not crazy," "trust your feelings," "you've made good decisions in the past so trust your wisdom," "you don't have to be perfect to be loved," "it's okay to make mistakes," "treat yourself gently," "tell me who it is and I'll go beat them up," and other helpful things like that. She also says, "You're a good person, a fine human being, and I love you."

We've talked more lately because both of us are dealing with a lot of pain in our lives; we're dealing with it in healthy, life-gracing kinds of ways which means it hurts even more and we need to cry and laugh it out.

She lets me laugh in the face of pain when nothing else seems to work, or when being serious just gets to be too much.

She's good at laughing, too; one of the few people who isn't shocked by my irreverent, cynical, tongue-in-cheek humor when it's at its best - or worst - depending upon how you look at it. She even finds cards that have the same off-beat way of viewing life that gives me permission to be as outrageous as I like if I need to – at least when I'm with her.

A while ago I asked for her help when I was facing a day of heartbreak. I asked her to come to our house to answer the phone while we were away for a couple of hours. She came and answered the phone, waited 'til we returned, took one look at me, and left.

She didn't say, "I think you should talk about it," or "How did it go?" or "How can I help?" or anything like that. She just left, knowing that there are times when that is the most loving thing to do.

We've learned to be honest with each other, the terrible-wonderful kind of honesty that let's us say hard things to one another about one another. We've pushed each other to take one more step, and then one more, in the direction of growth, fearful some times that it's been too much, but grateful always when the push has paid off.

She doesn't make promises easily, but when she does, she keeps them. And she's just beginning to understand how wonderful she is.

I wish I could rent her out to the world. It would be a better place.

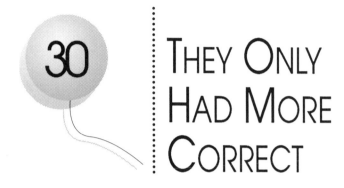

CHAPTER THIRTY

THEY ONLY HAD MORE CORRECT

When I returned to college after our youngest was in first grade, it was especially important to me that I do well, partly to justify the time and money spent, and partly to convince myself that becoming a student in my late thirties was not a foolish dream.

When I heard that the course Healthful Living, offered through the psychology department, would fulfill a general education requirement as well as provide some excellent stress management information, I jumped at the chance to take it.

There were three of us non-traditional students in the class, and we studied together in fear. The teacher was demanding; his assignments were complex and his tests were sheer torture. He was also a well-respected, excellent teacher that we came to esteem as well as fear.

His first test was awful, and most of us left the class feeling unsure of our performance. It didn't help our confidence any that we three older students were among the last to finish.

When he handed the tests back individually, face down so no one saw the grading and comments, our tension mounted. It reached a summit when he posted the curve on the board. Groans and sighs came from all parts of the room.

"Well now, let's talk about the test results. About a sixth of the class did quite well on the test. What can you tell about those people who did well?" With that he began to list on the board those characteristics that the class attributed to the people who did well: intelligent; hardworking; willing to give up other things in order to study; self-disciplined; self-motivated; persistent. Our teacher seemed to enjoy the assessments and continued to write until every possible adjective had been offered that would describe that group.

Then he did the same for the group who had done poorly. On and on we went listing the characteristics of those who had poor test results.

When it was all over, our instructor wiped his chalky hands onto the back of his jeans and said in a quiet voice, "The only thing you can tell about the people who did well on the test is that they answered more questions correctly than those who did poorly."

That was our first lesson in many about how our perceptions can influence the way we see ourselves and the world around us. We were encouraged to become aware of how we defined ourselves and challenged to develop broader perceptions of who we were and could be.

It didn't seem to make much sense at first, but as I spent more time examining myself, I realized that in order to survive in our complex and rapidly changing world, we need a variety of ways of seeing ourselves and a number of settings where we believe we can be happy.

Futurists predict that people entering the job market in the near future will likely hold eight to ten distinctly different jobs within a lifetime. Those jobs may utilize similar skills, but they will be different occupations, not simply different places of employment. In that kind of world, the more narrowly we define ourselves, the less likely we will be to find personal satisfaction.

When I think of someone who captures my imagination with her flexible image, I think of Linda. She's lean and attractive. She talks with her hands and in much detail. She's been a social worker, a full time homemaker, a student, a worker.

She's an accomplished seamstress and a dedicated mother, someone whose interests are broad and varied. When she was thinking about returning to school for something other than social work, I encouraged her to pursue what she really hoped to do, letting her know the ways our family had survived a similar situation.

It wasn't an easy decision, because her children were younger than ours at the time. But she held fast to her dream, and her husband was supportive. Eventually she headed off for two years of school.

She was a conscientious student, more serious than a number of the younger students in the class, and it was soon evident that she would excel. She received special recognition at graduation and returned home to relish her open house.

Linda looked radiant that day; laughing, relieved, and proud of what her whole family had done in order for her to have completed school. It was fun to see her look so good, and fun to watch her receive congratulations from the group.

Gradually I began to recognize some of her classmates, mostly because the first time they saw her on entering the house, they literally stopped in their tracks. You see, Linda had followed her dream to become a carpenter and had finished an intensive, difficult, two year course at a nearby vocational-technical school. Her classmates had never seen her in anything other than sturdy workclothes designed to keep out the Minnesota cold.

Linda now works for a construction company building houses. She doesn't dress nearly as nicely for work as when she's at home, and when she goes shopping for work clothes, she heads for departments in which most of us have never been.

Had Linda allowed herself to remain bound by the usual perceptions about women and what they do, what's feminine and what isn't, or what other people might think, I doubt she would have found the courage to persist in her carpentry schooling.

Linda lacked the role models that allow many of us to try something new. There weren't any women carpenters around to teach her. Instead, Linda paid attention to the things she found herself drawn to, small projects around the house, working with her father building a deck, and other minor carpentry jobs.

She thought, assessed, talked, took a deep breath, and plunged into a whole new area of life. She was freed to do so by a flexible view of herself and what is possible.

Linda may not always be a carpenter. For the time that she is, she's doing something she thoroughly enjoys, something that challenges her body and mind. She's doing something that allows her perfectionism to result in the highest quality finished project. She's learned a skill that she uses freely around the house.

More importantly, she provides a powerful lesson to her three children and anyone else paying attention. Life can be as rich and varied as we will allow ourselves to make it, even if we have to let go of some limiting perceptions in the process.

CHAPTER THIRTY ONE

Kristy's Friends

W hen I worked for Sacred Heart Parish, my office was in St. Mary's School. I shared a hall there with third and fourth graders. Sometimes I would slip into church on the days students were the main participants in the mass. They brought a freshness and sincerity to the worship I found enjoyable food for thought.

The theme of one of those masses for children was "Friends," and the kids chose appropriate scripture readings and psalm refrains to emphasize the importance of friends and the quality that friendships should have. Even the songs captured the essence of friendship. It was obvious the kids related to the theme. Friendship was a concept familiar and dear to them, one that they could grasp and make their own.

After communion, the children sat for a moment of reflection. That was when I noticed a young girl slip from her place and make her way to the front of the church, a piece of paper in hand. The first thing I noticed about her was her bearing. She held herself with an erect yet relaxed posture that might have been described as reserved, but for her youth.

I learned later that her name was Kristy and that she was in third grade. At the time I knew only that there was a quality about her that caught and held my attention.

Kristy stepped to the lectern and adjusted the microphone. After the children were settled, she looked out over the group without smiling but without seeming self-conscious, took a breath, and in a low voice filled with simplicity and sincerity, read the following communion reflection that she had written especially for the mass on friends.

Friends are people who are nice. People who are nice have the most friends. Like Jesus said, "Love one another as I have loved you." People like it when friends say, "thank you;" "please;" "come and play;" "I like you;" and, "you are my friend."

People don't like it when friends say things like, "I don't like you anymore;" "you can't come to my party;" "leave me alone;" and, "don't touch me." Those kinds of words will hurt someone's feelings. So if you want to be a good friend be nice like Jesus would want us to be.

When she was finished she calmly returned to her place, none of the smiling or giddiness typical of third graders who have just "performed," no glancing around to gauge the reactions to what she had done. No, Kristy simply walked back to her place and sat down, seeming to be content to have offered her best for the mass.

Kristy gave people the feeling she had already experienced both the joys and pains of friendship and had put a lot of thought into what she said. At an early age, she seemed wise about the ways of treating others

I've also known new parents who have seemed wise about the ways of treating their children. Without falling into the trap of trying to be friends with their children in inappropriate ways, they have treated their children as they would a valued friend.

We know a couple who worked with their daughter from the beginning to help her identify and acknowledge her feelings. In their household, if Katy was crying, one of them might say, "Katy, you seem sad," or angry, or frustrated, or whatever seemed to fit the situation. They would do the same in public. After listening to her efforts to explain her feelings, they asked her what she thought would be helpful for her at the time.

They didn't jerk her around, tell her to stop making such a fuss, argue away her feelings or shame her for such nonsense. When her actions looked more like temper out of control, they set limits for her, providing a time-out that included the need to talk about the situation when she felt more in control.

Whenever I was with the three of them, I marveled at how good it felt. There was a feeling of respect for one another that brought a sense of peace to the household. They seemed to say by their actions that children and adults were equally valued in their household even though children might be lacking in wisdom or experience.

Too often I've been in situations that are just the opposite of that. Parents have berated, ridiculed, corrected and punished their children publicly in ways that have made me sick to my stomach. I've done the same myself and known each time that it was wrong.

When Kristy put together her reflection for the children's mass, I doubt she had enough life experience to tell parents to treat their children with the same consideration as they would their best friend. But she certainly understood the essence of that kind of caring.

Friendship of the kind Kristy described means giving the other person the benefit of the doubt, and saying openly and often that they are appreciated and special.

Wouldn't it be great if we all could do those things with the same grace and gentleness that Kristy showed when she walked to the pulpit to share the wisdom of her young heart.

CHAPTER THIRTY TWO

TOO GOOD TO BELIEVE

I wrote a reference letter awhile ago for someone who'll be graduating this year. He's a neat kid, someone I've come to respect, admire, and enjoy. Even so, it took the better part of a week, thinking on and off about what to say, and an hour writing it, before the letter seemed correct. Reference letters aren't easy for me. I want to be honest without overstating the situation, yet I know that there is certain "reference language" that can cause everyone to sound about the same. Reference letters aren't supposed to be too long, yet capturing a person's character and personality doesn't lend itself to a few quick paragraphs. So I struggled, discarded, edited, and finally said, "It's done."

With the letter stored in my computer's memory, I asked my young friend to read it and see if he could live with it, or if it needed some minor changes before being official. It was a positive letter, a good recommendation. It was also honest. The smile that appeared on the young man's face when he finished the letter said he liked it too. Then he said something that has been food for thought ever since. "I'm not *that* good," he said, with both modesty and conviction. I sensed he was not only speaking for himself but for each of us who hears true, positive praise about the kind of person we are.

I'm not talking about compliments. Many of us have worked at becoming gracious accepters of compliments. It's become possible for us to hear, "You did a good job on that," or, "You look really nice today," without being uncomfortable about it or having to deny it. Letters of reference or recommendation are different, however. They focus on the total person and cover not just one good quality, but many, and people are often uncomfortable if they read letters of recommendation about themselves.

If the young man who had felt uncomfortable with how good he sounded in the reference letter I wrote would have had to read only one sentence of the letter, I think he would have had to agree with any one of the individual sentences. Yet, when it was all put together, it seemed too much.

What I wanted to tell him then, and didn't, is that yes, he is *that* good, probably not all the time, with every person, or under all circumstances. But the qualities I have come to know and appreciate in him are real and deserve to be mentioned.

None of us are as good, all the time, as a positive letter of recommendation would cause us to appear. We all have hidden faults and attitudes that we would not want shared with the world. We commonly rein in our negative impulses, ones that might surprise or shock people if they were known, in order to live in harmony with others. We also have failings that aren't at all hidden.

Still, most of us are truly wonderful people, rough edges and all, and I wish each one of us could have a letter of recommendation written about us every other month or so. We deserve to see, in black and white, the goodness that others see in us. Even when we live in supportive situations where we get compliments and other signs of being appreciated, it's rare that we would hear the full range of another's regard for us. Sometimes seeing that full range can be important.

Most of us could compose a negative letter of reference about ourselves with no trouble at all, except possibly being unable to keep it brief. We all need the positive information others have about us to balance our negative self-awareness. The key is to be able to live with the paradox that we are all a mixture of the wonderful and the non-wonderful. We all have impulses for great nobility and considerable evil. That doesn't diminish the fact that we are wonderful and worthy of being told about it.

Some of the good things said to me about qualities people appreciated have become cherished memories. These memories encourage me on days when I'm down and serve as models for me when I strive to be better. How wonderful it would be for all of us to have a written "letter of recommendation" that could be tucked away and brought out from time to time, to be cherished like a favorite letter from a friend.

It needn't worry us that it might be only part of the picture or that we might get conceited if we believed and liked it. We have so many opportunities to experience what we lack that it wouldn't hurt us to see and know how good we are. Besides, until we know our goodness, it's difficult to make peace with our not-so-good qualities, and learning to be gentle and compassionate with others requires us to know the shadow side of who we are.

And so I would tell my young friend to make a copy of his recommendation letter and read it over until it fits like an old shoe. I'd tell him to work at learning to celebrate the goodness that other people see in him and to be thankful for his capacity to touch others lives in meaningful, enjoyable ways.

33

Our Rightful Inheritance

My parents' generation lived with many standards and hopes that are quite different from ours. One thing important to them and many of their friends was the ability to leave an inheritance for their children, a sum of money they could pass on when they died that represented their love and devotion.

Many people that age, and the generation before them, worked hard and sacrificed not only to provide for the immediate needs of their children but also to provide an inheritance. When I was a social worker at our local hospital, I listened to many people in crisis because their hospital bills were going to eat up money that had been saved for their children's inheritance.

Some people have offered their children money at a time when it was needed, making the offer by saying, "I can give you your inheritance money now if you need it." People who have accepted such offers say that they deeply appreciated the use of that money when the need was so critical.

Sometimes growing up with the notion of an inheritance in the future has caused people to believe that they "have it coming," that simply by virtue of being in that family they have a right to an inheritance, no strings attached. The term birthright takes on a meaning close to that: by virtue of my birth I have a right to some of what you have.

I was recently part of a day-long workshop designed to offer information and encouragement to women who found themselves in situations that needed to be changed or who wanted more for themselves. In preparing for that talk, I did a lot of thinking about what we have a right to expect from life, what we were intended for, and what our human "inheritance" is to be.

I believe that we have been given a "birthright" to be healthy and whole; that we were intended to live full, peace-filled lives free from fear. Our desire to be mentally, physically, spiritually or emotionally healthy and nourished, is a sign that we are aware of our birthright.

Too often, however, when people begin to experience dissatisfaction in their lives, when they begin to recognize unhealthy patterns of behaving or unhealthy relationships, they question their right to seek change because they think they're being selfish. It's true that being selfish is part of being human, and that, as humans, we often won't recognize when we're being selfish. But wanting life to be better or healthier is not being self-indulgent.

If we're serious about trying to live responsibly, we're likely to recognize selfish patterns developing in our lives or agree with assessments from others we respect. More commonly, we end up labeling our yearning for rightful change as being selfish, either out of conditioning or a desire to avoid taking the necessary risks to improve our lives.

It's not selfish to want a better life for ourselves and others; it's a want born of the dignity due the human person. It's not selfish to want to be valued and cherished, listened to and included, or able to develop our talents and abilities and be recognized for our uniqueness. These are birthrights, our human inheritance. We should be able to receive them from birth, rather than at death.

Because of the nature of things, few of us have or

will receive all of these as infants and children. Sometimes this causes lifelong pain. Sometimes it results in development of self-defeating behavior patterns. Regardless, inner urgings to make life better are urgings to be trusted and acted on, because it's our birthright and responsibility to be whole and healthy, to have lives of meaning and purpose.

It's our birthright to experience life to the full and be able to share that wealth with others. It's our birthright to be able to create a better world — and to start doing so with our own lives.

CHAPTER THIRTY FOUR

A WALL THAT SOOTHES

F eeling pain, frustration, and irritation with myself and life in general, I sat down one day in our living room to stew and fret. This admittedly accomplishes little, but it's what I was doing.

At some point I realized I was focusing on the artwork on our wall. The memories and thoughts it evoked were soothing, comforting, and helping make things okay.

I was looking at a serigraph done by Alice Ottinger and Jean Zamboni of the OZ Press. It's a field in winter with ice crystals and snow chunks caught in weeds.

The OZ Press is a fascinating place for me, and I frequently haul visitors there to see "art in progress." Jean and Alice have been on several college faculties, among other things, and besides being frequent award winners, they are symbols of self-reliance, determination in the face of opposition, cooperation, and a studied appreciation of life. Those are good qualities to ponder, and having their "Snow Pops" on my wall helps remind me to do that.

Our main living room wall has a "collage." It's an assortment of things hung together because there aren't enough walls to hang them separately. The largest piece on that wall behind the couch is a country scene of a broken farm wagon in a field of golden grasses, with the hint of an abandoned building in the background.

It was done by a local artist, Mike Smith, when he was still in college. It's a quiet, soothing piece that captures the reverence for the land we felt moving to a rural community from the larger city. It also reminds me of the emotion felt buying artwork from Mike, a college junior at the time, who was still new enough at his profession to feel awed that people wanted to pay money for his work.

Next to the country scene is a small metal cross, and then a crosscut of a branch with the bark attached. A tin butterfly rests in it and also a tiny metal plaque, no larger than a postage stamp that reads, "If any man will come after me, let him deny himself and let him take up his cross and follow me."

It was a Christmas present from our son, years back, and I remember his eagerness for me to open it. We'd given the kids a list of ideas to help them shop. He'd happened upon the plaque by accident, while shopping alone. "Open it," he said, practically dancing, and I knew it was important to him because he'd left one of his own presents unwrapped to come stand by me while I opened it.

"As soon as I saw it I knew you'd love it," he said after with a joyful confidence that took my breath away. I treasure it still, remembering the special glow Philip felt at having chosen a surprise gift that I would cherish.

Just beneath it is a print of a rugged-looking man with his head thrown back in a full laugh. It's called "Jesus Christ-Liberator," a powerful reminder to me of the fullness of life we're intended to have and the liberation that comes from risking to live life fully.

Next is another work by Mike Smith, a small metal etching of a young boy standing next to a gumball machine. His head is down, hands hanging dejectedly at his side. Clearly, he knows the wonder of gumballs, and he has no penny. He serves to remind me of all the times in my life that have been filled with the ache of knowing, wanting, and being without.

Beneath it is a calligraphy print. The center reads, "All things have their season, and in their times, all things pass under heaven." Written in a circle surrounding the saying is the remainder of Ecclesiastes 3:1-9. Too often, in my impatience, I want today, this season, to be the time that everything is completed or resolved. The print serves as a gentle slow-down that I've come to cherish.

Next are three quick plaques; the first a "Peace to all who enter here," then a boy squatting at the ocean's edge gazing at shells. An Einstein quote says, "The important thing is not to stop questioning," and it reminds me of the richness in my life that has come from a curious mind and encouragement as a kid to ask questions until I was satisfied. Even though my desire for knowledge is so strong some days it hurts, the plaque reminds me I can continue to question 'til the day I die.

Beneath it is a plaque that was wood-burned by a friend after Dad died. It says, "I will never forget you, my people, I have carved you on the palm of my hand." It speaks to me of friendship, hope, and immortality.

The final piece is another by Jean Zamboni. It's a partial figure on a horse in a field that encompasses all four seasons of nature. It reminds me of wanting to be present to all the seasons of my life, as doer not spectator.

Over the years, I've come to realize that my surroundings need to speak to me of things I consider important. And so, the collage that would give a decorator fits holds rich memories and lessons for me. It serves to soothe and comfort or challenge me, to center me again when life gets crazy and I determine to fret, stew and try to solve all life's problems in a day.

The only thing the wall is missing is a quick punch of humor. Someday I'll add that.

CHAPTER THIRTY FIVE

A Rich Return

Her name was Mabel and we met her at Wilder Nursing Home in St. Paul on an Easter Sunday morning years ago. She was sitting and eating her dinner at the same table as my husband's aunt. Jim's Aunt Esther was a private person, not given to chatting with people she didn't know well, so mostly she just nodded and smiled at Mabel. Mabel, too, seemed private, but eventually we exchanged brief bits of conversation.

She had never married and her relatives lived out East. She'd taught kindergarten for thirty-one years and treasured those times. She said that very day was her ninety-first birthday. By then, the dinner table included Jim and me, Aunt Esther, Mabel, our son, our youngest daughter, and our Italian AFS student. For a moment we were all silent, each reacting to what it might be like to be ninety-one. Then we all talked at once, congratulating her and asking questions.

Not long after that, she finished eating and got up to return to her room. Her arthritis made standing difficult, and she nearly pulled the table over in her struggle to get up, but her manner told us she didn't want help. She thanked us for our birthday wishes and slowly walked off.

Jim immediately called over one of the dining room workers. Was it really Mabel's ninety-first birthday or was she confused? Could someone that age really be so alert and pleasant? The worker was new, so we searched out the calendar in the elevator. Mabel had been right; we knew then that we had to do something to make that day special for her.

Should we divide Aunt Esther's candy with her? That didn't seem right; Esther's gift was for Esther. Make a card? Nice, but not hardly enough for a ninety-first birthday that falls on an Easter Sunday. Go to her room and sing Happy Birthday? Fun, but not enough to satisfy the sheer joy of surprise that was building in us. Jim and Esther headed back to Aunt Esther's room while the rest of us piled into the car for a present hunt.

We were only blocks from downtown, but because it was Easter Sunday, virtually no businesses were open. Thank goodness for convenience gas stations. A quick run through one yielded us nothing but a close-to-dead hyacinth plant in petrified soil, and concern was mounting because we needed to be at my mom's house on time for Easter dinner!

We ran back out into the car, stumbling over each other, and headed to another gas station eighteen blocks away. We found better plants in better soil, made a quick purchase, and returned to the nursing home with spirits high. A stop at the nurse's station yielded paper and magic markers. Our daughter Monica created the card while Jim and Esther approved the gift, and we plotted our approach.

Which was her room? Esther thought it was next door. Wrong name. With no nurses readily available, we made a flying trip downstairs to the main floor registry to find Mabel's name and room number. Then the six of us started off down the hall with plant and card in hand, whispering and laughing, to get to her private room.

We grew suddenly silent outside her door, straining to hear the sounds from within that might indicate she was there. Quiet greeted us, and for a moment we feared she might have gone out. We knocked twice, heard a quiet, "Come in," and then all six of us entered her room singing "Happy Birthday."

She was lying on her bed. She pulled herself up slowly on a trapeze which hung there to assist her, took in the sight of us, and responded with a smile of dignity and grace that stole our hearts. She said she'd had a visitor from church but then had lain down to take a nap believing her birthday celebration was over. Now we had made it special.

We hugged her and gave her the plant. She read the homemade card from us as if it were in gold leaf, commenting on each of the things Monica had drawn to make it festive. We chatted for just a minute, she thanked us, and we left. We'd given her a plant and a card. She'd given us a sense of significance.

We talked often about Mabel for the first few days after our little celebration, then again upon receiving a gracious handwritten thank-you from her a couple weeks later. Those moments of brief celebration gave each of us the feeling that we mattered.

Our group of six, who walked the nursing home hall that Easter Sunday morning to celebrate the ninety-first birthday of Mabel, represented 215 years of living. Within a thirty minute period of time, our gifting Mabel resulted in her giving us all a sense of significance that will last as long as the memory.

That's not a bad return for our efforts.

CHAPTER THIRTY SIX

A REALITY CHECK

This is a crazy time in history to be alive, trying to balance the need to be there for others with the need to take care of oneself. Several years ago I was confronted with the mess I was making of balancing my life and came to conclusions about some important matters. The ongoing challenge for me is to slow down and trust in my wisdom.

After six months of working for Steele County in the child protection unit, I decided to get some short term counseling. I was dealing with critical situations in my job, and I wanted help sorting out some of my own unfinished issues so I wouldn't complicate already complicated situations.

During one counseling session, I mentioned the needs of one of my children and my feeling of inadequacy. With that the counselor said, "What do *you* need?," repeating the question when I made no response. I remember trying to make light of the situation, joking that I didn't need anything. I left the question unanswered.

It plagued me. I could think of things that Jim and the kids needed for a sense of peace and happiness in their lives, and I could also come up with lists of needs that my friends and clients had. But a list for myself just wasn't anywhere in my thoughts. I realized with surprise and some dismay that I had gotten so caught up with doing for others, I was no longer in touch with myself.

Though I tried hard, the particulars for a list of my needs wouldn't come, other than generalities like "I need to feel loved and fulfilled." About five days later, this is what I jotted down on a piece of scratch paper:

alone
exercise
companionship
order
affection
creative outlet
prayer/spiritual reading
nurture
intimacy
communication/feedback
professional outlet

They hadn't flowed in any particular rank or order, but I was grateful the thoughts had finally come. Then I took a good hard look at the list and felt lousy. As I examined the items on my needs list, I saw examples of how I had allowed working, wifing, and mothering to become so important that I wasn't fulfilling some basic needs of my own life.

I had to do battle with the notion that taking care of myself was selfish. It also scared me to realize that no one but me was responsible for my health and happiness. It left me with no one to blame when my life got truly chaotic.

I'm still not able to schedule my life in the way I might like; there are simply too many variables at this time. But paying attention to my list establishes some balance between my physical, spiritual, social and emotion needs. I'm more peaceful, productive, and enjoyable to be around.

It's meant having to get my particular values quite

clear in my mind, however, because even with the best list and plan, time demands of today outnumber what's available. Without a sense of what's really important in my life, what my long range and short range goals are, it's too easy for me to get fragmented. I respond to things that seem vital at the time but are really based on someone else's list of priorities.

I've come to realize that when I start getting "crazy": overeating, perfectionist, self-pitying, procrastinating, feeling overly responsible and overly important, or being somewhat immobilized and doing little or nothing, it's time for me to take out my list and do an inventory.

Invariably, I find that my life has become clearly lopsided. I'm overly focused in one area, overly involved in taking care of other people, or simply unrealistic about how much can be accomplished in one day.

I've found ways to combine the things that I need. Brisk walks with a friend serve my needs for exercise and intimacy. Spiritual reading and reflection, done alone, in the early morning quiet of our house answer other needs. Writing can soothe my need for creativity and provide a professional outlet. Volunteering hospice care allows me further use of my social work skills, as well as time to nurture others. Well-planned time with Jim can also fulfill many of these needs.

Mostly, I've learned I'm responsible for how my life unfolds, and how well I cope with it depends on how well I listen to my inner needs. Marked imbalance in any area over too long a period of time takes its toll in unhealthy ways.

Often, I need to remind myself that I'm physical, spiritual, social, emotional, and intellectual, an interplay of qualities woven together as finely as the most intricate tapestry. It's a tapestry fashioned with the help of others, to be sure, but one in which I direct the final pattern and richness.

CHAPTER THIRTY SEVEN

LISTENING TO LOSS

Not long ago, I heard of a person's anguish at the inability of friends to comfort him when a new friend of his committed suicide.

He said he'd gone to a bar a couple nights after the funeral to be with regular buddies and have a chance to talk about his loss. His friends knew he had suffered trauma at the recent death, and he had hopes of being able to talk about the meaning of that person's life, and his shock that such a thing could have happened.

After an hour of listening to his buddies discuss hunting and debate the merits of steel shot versus lead shot, he left in shock and pain to try to handle his need for comfort in some other way.

Later, I heard a grief counselor talk about visiting a man on the anniversary of his wife's death. The man expressed his gratefulness for the counselor's time, saying, "You have spoken my wife's name more in the past two hours than all my friends have in the past six months."

As touching as both those stories are, it's safe to say that neither of these men had cold, uncaring friends with blatant disregard for the feelings of others. It's far more likely that neither group of friends knew what to do to help someone grieve, so they did the kindest thing they knew. They provided some diversion to help their friend get his mind off the loss.

Unfortunately, life doesn't work that way for most of us who mourn the loss of someone or something we've held dear. Grief has a way of preoccupying, a way of demanding that we go over and over the details of the loss in our minds and hearts. The loss we experienced is a wound in need of healing. But unlike physical wounding, which can heal with the benefit of pain-killing medication, the wound of loss requires experiencing the pain of grief in order for its healing to occur.

That means tears, talking, sorting through belongings, rereading cards, and feeling the pain of familiar yet empty places are all a part of the healing process. It means that people doing necessary grieving may appear out of control, self-pitying, morbid, or obsessed with thoughts of their loss.

In years gone by, grieving people used to wear black arm bands during a period of mourning. Most people are grateful society has progressed beyond that point, but possibly we eliminated a simple way of identifying people who needed extra time and attention

Friends have shared with me the loneliness and emptiness of having suffered a loss that no one seems to ask about except in the first days after the funeral. They've said that while they wouldn't want everyone they talk to bringing up the subject, there are people close enough to add to their burden by not asking how they're doing. Grieving people have said they'd at least like the option of talking about their loss, but feel it's almost impossible unless someone gives them an entry point into the conversation by mentioning it first.

"We don't always want to talk about the loss," they say, "and sometimes we tell people we'd rather talk about something else, but it's helpful when someone asks, and gives us the choice."

What does that mean for those of us standing on the sidelines through someone else's loss? If talking about loss helps a person heal, how can we be a part of that in ways that are respectful and humane?

We can ask, "How are you doing? I heard about the death of your mother and I'm sorry," and then we can be quiet to listen to what follows. If it's been awhile since the event of loss, we can say, "How's it going for you these days?," and not be quick to change the conversation if they should say they're doing fine. Sometimes it's hard for people to tell whether that's a sincere question or just a routine greeting not really intended to start a conversation.

If someone starts talking about their loss, there are responses which can encourage them to continue: "Say more about that," "what's that like for you?," or, "I didn't know your husband very well. Tell me about him." Sometimes just nodding and sitting without speaking will encourage the other person to continue.

What doesn't help is for the listener to offer advice or describe what they did in a similar situation. There may be a time for that kind of help, but usually it's best when it's asked for, or when it's many months after the loss.

Initially, the grieving person just needs to talk, to go over the details and what they should or shouldn't have done, time and again, both for the reality to sink in and for the pain to come out.

What's more common is that those who listen feel the need to reassure. We forget, or never learned, that there's an illogic about grieving which causes perfectly intelligent people to say things they'd never say otherwise. Even so, they don't need correcting, or having their convoluted thinking made to make sense. They just need to talk without having set things straight.

Sometimes when people talk about their loss they begin to cry, and we're convinced that we've made matters worse by making that person sad. Tears simply confirm feelings already there, feelings that need to be experienced as part of healing's pain.

Sometimes people talk about their losses perfectly dry-eyed. We wonder then if we've been of any help because they're obviously doing so well they don't need to be reminded of their loss. There's no rule about crying and grief; everyone should be allowed to cry, but no one should be required to cry. People are as individual in their grief as they are in other aspects of their life, and public tears may or may not be a part of their style.

It's not helpful to repeat religious cliches for the comfort of others. People with faith already believe, and people without will not be helped. It's one thing if the person who is grieving shares spirituality that has been sustaining; it's another if we're trying to provide something for them to hold on to.

It's also not helpful to say, "How old was your mother?," and then, "She lived a full life." When someone has lost a parent, regardless of the age, they've lost their past. They begin to know what it means to be an orphan, and need to have their loss acknowledged, not diminished by suggestions that the loss of an elderly parent isn't significant.

Again, if the grieving person says their parent lived a full life, or was elderly, that's fine; but it's not a useful or comforting comment coming from someone else.

Cards and letters, quiet listening, and reminders of anniversaries or special times are helpful. Silence, diverted conversations, and medications intended to dull pain are not.

It's a blessing that we can learn how to help one another in pain. As with the mastering of any skill, we will feel awkward and uncomfortable, scared and doubtful in the learning. But listening caringly to another person's grief is a skill to be acquired, not a trait some people are born with, and our efforts will bring untold reward.

CHAPTER THIRTY EIGHT

THE AFFECTION OF YOUTH

E ach year when school starts I'm reminded of the saying, "It is no small matter to have won the affection of a child." It causes me to think of our son's third grade teacher.

Philip had a difficult second grade year that included being ridiculed by his teacher and being sent to the principal's office on a number of occasions as a form of discipline. We tried to intervene and establish a working relationship with his teacher, but though things improved some, the year was a hard one for Phil and the entire family.

He entered third grade shy and apprehensive, and our feelings at home were similar. We watched him try to compensate for not feeling very good about himself in school, watched him put on a bravado that looked sadly macho and unlike him. We tried to explain that other people might not see the real Phil if he acted too much that way. Mostly we just hoped and prayed that he wouldn't have a second consecutive year of painful school experience.

We tried not to seem too eager to know how things were going for him once third grade started, but it was always on our minds. Then somewhere into the first month of school we realized that Phil was sharing stories about school at dinnertime. He was talking about clever plays on words his teacher had constructed, projects in the classroom, and appealing things he had learned. Before long we realized that Phil was crazy about his teacher, and she was crazy about him.

Her affection seemed unconditional; she was able to effectively discipline Phil and still let him know that she genuinely liked him. Phil blossomed in her classroom, gaining a sense of himself that we alone could never have provided. I can't think of her without a deep gratitude that sometimes brings a sting of tears.

I had someone like that in my life, a couple who were friends of my parents. I never went to their house to visit them, but whenever they were at our house, usually with a group of adults, they sought me out to ask me what was happening in my life. And they really listened. During the time they were with me they were totally focused on me, not on the party. We held serious conversations in various corners of the rec room, conversations about my fears, about my larger questions of life, about some of my successes. Sometimes all they did was banter with me.

Through it all, I came to understand that they loved me unconditionally. No matter what kind of mistakes or stupid things I might do, what they saw in me went much deeper. I could always count on them to care about me and welcome me. Over the years, I've clung to the memory of their unconditional love, and used it to sustain me through difficult times of self doubt and uncertainty.

At this point in my life I know two things are certain: we don't raise our children alone, and every kid needs someone, other than a parent, to think they are wonderful. Teachers can do that, so can parents of friends, and neighbors who are interested and available. There are coaches, youth group leaders, and bosses who can reflect back to kids their innate worth in ways that parents sometimes cannot.

Whenever an adult has an honest, caring interest in a young person, the chance for growth and goodness is present. That interest creates a climate where young people are willing to be known and where they will listen to the wisdom of adults that is shared, not through advice or preaching, but through the telling of life's experiences and meaning.

The amazing thing about that kind of regard is that young people today often find ways to express their gratitude for having been esteemed by an adult. This creates an unforgettable bond.

It truly is no small thing to have won the affection of a child.

CHAPTER THIRTY NINE

THE VOICE OF GOD

I was asked to preach on an Old Testament story about a boy named Samuel, as part of an afternoon ecumenical Lenten worship service held at the local Episcopal Church. These services had been a tradition at St. Paul's for years, and the people who preached were members of the ministerial association.

I prepared for the day well aware that I was not seminary-trained, nor an ordained clergy person. I was a laywoman employed as a parish worker. This concerned me because a number of people coming to the service would be more interested in "experts" interpretations than my opinions about the passage I was to preach on.

On the other hand, I had neither the time nor resources at hand to do a scholarly study of Samuel. So I read the story over a number of times and decided to present what seemed true to me from my life experience. Scripture is as much a story of us and our relationship with an all-loving God, as it is a story about ancient people and their God.

In the story, Samuel is a boy, serving an older, wiser Eli. In the night, Samuel hears someone calling. Believing it is Eli, he goes to him to be of assistance. Twice the voice calls in the night; twice Eli is awakened only to say he hadn't called. On the third time that Samuel goes to

Eli, Eli recognizes that it must be God calling. He instructs Samuel to go back to sleep, but if he hears the voice again to respond, "Speak, Lord, your servant is listening."

It occurred to me that many of us mistake the gentle callings of God in the night: our innermost longings, our urgings, our restlessness. I believe we have a God-created space within that can only be filled through relationship with Him. I also believe we frequently mistake the longing that space creates, and like Samuel, respond in the wrong places.

The story about Samuel says he was not familiar with the Lord because the Lord had not revealed Himself to him yet. Likewise, many of us have grown up in Christian families that adhere to Christian values and faith, but we don't make those truly our own until well into adulthood. We're familiar with the Lord in a general sort of way, but not in a way that allows a more clear recognition of His call.

So when God calls in the night, we seek our identity and comfort somewhere else: in possessions, career, relationships, addictions, and activity that leaves us still searching in the daylight.

I believe many of God's calls are gentle and gradual. Some people can't hear them because they've suffered experiences at other people's hands that have to be healed before they can sense God's tender beckoning.

One of the first ways that God calls us to Himself is in the stirrings of self love, out of the gradual recognition that we are valued and lovable and worthwhile simply because we are.

He calls to us by drawing us into relationships with others where we can learn about ourselves and provide others with knowledge about themselves. Through these relationships, we can gain strength and enthusiasm to journey together and make God's kingdom real on earth.

I also believe we are gradually called to recognize the God within, to understand that the God who bound Himself to us in an everlasting love is not in the sky, creation, or a church building. He is nested within us, a God-reality and a God-space that will never be filled with anything else.

I believe all this because I believe the calling of Samuel that Eli recognized as being God, the calling to which there really is no other response but, "Speak Lord, your servant is listening," is a call to surrender to the eternal, incomparable, and unconditional love of God.

We're familiar with contracts. We agree to do something, and the other person agrees to do something. As long as both parties do their part, the contract remains valid. When I buy a car, I agree to a certain number of payments on a certain schedule. As long as I fulfill my part of the contract, I get to keep and drive the car. When I don't, the bank repossesses the car.

God's love isn't like that. It's called a covenanted love. He says, "I have made you for myself; you are mine. I chose you before you were knit in your mother's womb. I have carved your name on the palm of my hand. You will be mine for all time ... ours is an everlasting love. You did not choose me, I chose you. I have called you by name."

And he adds, "There is nothing you could ever do that would end my love for you. Nothing." And then He says, "If you are willing to listen to me, if you will trust what you hear, if you will try to clear the pathways to make room for my voice, I will speak words of love to you that you will not be able to resist."

And I think God says, "Trust even in your responding in confusion to the wrong places, because if you listen enough and respond enough, there will eventually be wisdom, either your own or that of someone like Eli who will be able to recognize your restlessness as the voice of God."

I think we have to want that to happen. We must ask to hear God's voice and be willing to do some things to help in hearing it. But the voice and relationship are God's doing, and we must trust in the process.

Once we learn to be open to the voice of God calling us to recognize his everlasting love, we will also begin to recognize the call to goodness and nobility; the call to service and caring that will make the voice of God real to others.

When that happens, it will be easier for us to respond, "Here I am, Lord; your servant is listening," with a trust that will make a difference in the world.

CHAPTER FORTY

UNEXPECTED BOUNTY

Owatonna is a city that clearly draws its life from agriculture. It's surrounded by rich farmland and much evidence of agribusiness. There's a strong 4-H program and record-winning Future Farmers of America that compete internationally.

A local canning company grows crops and cans high-quality vegetables. Throughout the growing season, it's common to see trucks haul various vegetables to the company for processing, starting in spring with asparagus and stretching into fall with the final handling of pumpkins.

Once every few years, one of the trucks will overturn due to a soft shoulder on a narrow road, a load that shifted on a sharp curve, or an inexperienced driver that pulled into the truck's path. Invariably, the vegetables spill out and become unfit for canning.

One year a corn truck overturned east of town, across from the home of a co-worker of mine. At coffee the next day she had wonderful stories to tell about strange movements in the night. It seemed that as sundown came and dusk turned to darkness, odd, bobbing lights began to show up in the fields surrounding her home.

Cars on the road became more numerous. They'd

slow down, some drivers turning off their headlights as their cars crept slowly forward, closer to the corn spill. Gradually it became clear that, in the anonymity of darkness, people were coming to help themselves to the riches provided by the canning company's mishap.

Our co-worker said it was quite a sight, especially when she figured out the bobbing lights were caused by flashlights, held in the hands of people sneaking through the fields, crouching low against the danger of detection.

They came with ice cream buckets, paper bags, backpacks, a wheelbarrow, and two carrying chest coolers. The people with cars had a variety of containers they used to nab the corn, and some just opened their trunks and began to toss in whatever corn they could get their hands on.

Somehow, that picture of the corn raid reminds me of life and the way people relate to its fullness. I'm a believer that life is intended to be lived to the full. My guess is that if we knew how abundant life and its experiences were meant to be, we'd each pull a piggyback semi up to life and load it full.

Instead, I see some people come to life's riches with a sandwich bag; they expect that much from life and no more. Others come with more sizeable containers, but they come alone in the dark of night, and slip away if anyone seems to notice. Others come, load up more than they can carry, and then leave some behind rather than ask for help carrying the load.

The ones I admire are the ones who come with a big container and a friend or two, as if on an adventure, wanting a full load, and willing to share.

The most wonderful part of the corn spill story is that unbeknownst to all the people who turned into thieves in the night, the canning company had announced over the radio that people were welcome to drive to the spill and help themselves to whatever amount they would like.

That's also a mirror of life. We're offered wonderful, unexpected, unearned abundance in life. We're offered take-it-in-the-daylight, share-it-with-your-friends abundance. It's not something to be taken for granted or treated carelessly, but it's there: a life of untold abundance, waiting for us to find the courage to fill ourselves full of its treasure.

CHAPTER FORTY ONE

USEFUL
MESSAGES

O nly an hour after chatting with a woman at a funeral dinner, I found myself kneeling in a ditch praying over her dead body. She had been in a fatal accident caused when a blinding sheet of snow was blown into the path of her car by a passing semi. Among other things, I decided then that I would no longer put off telling people the things I valued about them.

The woman was a stranger to me, and I had no way of knowing the quality of her relationships at the time she died. But I know it's easy to leave 'til tomorrow things that we might say today, especially what we value in one another.

Criticism and correction seems to come more easily, particularly when dealing with family members. Maybe we think it's important to help form behavior, or we take for granted that family members know we love them, anyway.

Even though criticism may be useful, some of the greatest growth I've experienced over the years has come from people who have shared what they appreciated about me. As often as I've tried to act indifferently, and even if I was embarrassed by positive comments, those words became special gifts I've held onto, thought about, and used to help form a picture of myself.

There's a story about a little boy and a birthday that

reminds me of the value of positive words. The young lad got a set of harmless darts as a gift, and after his friends had gone home, he and his mom were alone together. His mom, who was good at sharing fun said, "Let's play darts. We can take turns throwing."

The little boy, who was still dancing with the excitement of the party, wheeled around and said eagerly, "No. I'll throw, and you say, 'Wonderful!'"

Like the little boy, it's hard for us to ignore when a "wonderful," "you're neat," or "I think you're great" is directed toward us. "Nice job" goes a long way at helping us feel good about ourselves. For a long time it seemed that those kinds of words were enough for me, both to receive and express. After the death of the woman following the funeral dinner, however, I began to believe that more could be said. More words could be useful in helping ourselves and others come to a fuller self-understanding and appreciation.

"I like your enthusiasm," or, "your openness is great," gives a more complete message to someone than, "you're neat." Positive comments that identify an appreciated behavior or characteristic go a long way toward helping a person form a useful identity. Such specific comments may seem more risky to deliver, but they're worth the risk.

My sister-in-law gives seminars for people considering career changes. In these seminars, she assigns adult students the task of asking at least three friends or co-workers to define the student's strengths, skills, and abilities. Even though asking such questions is hard for most people, patterns of strengths often show up that are useful in career planning.

Many of us form new understandings about ourselves based on information we acquire as adults. Close friendships and work relationships can allow us to broaden the way we see ourselves and deepen our appreciation of the kind of person we've become.

Yet many of us formed our primary image of ourselves when we were children or teenagers. Those images depended on the assessment of people close to us. Kids and teens need adults around them, in addition to their parents, who think they're great. It's easier for that to happen when extended families live closer together, and aunts, uncles and grandparents are readily available with words of encouragement or positive feedback.

When teens and adults work side by side for long hours, some of the good information about one's worth gets passed back and forth as easily and as naturally as the sweat soaks their clothing. When adults spend more time away from home and teens spend more time in extracurricular activities, part-time jobs and leisure, it's much harder for that kind of information to be passed on.

Part-time jobs may provide income and occupational training for teens, but rarely do adult co-workers help them see what talents or special qualities they bring to that job. Even adult co-workers rarely share appreciation of specific qualities that they see in one another.

Hours spent sitting side by side watching videos don't teach us how to tell someone they make a difference. Likewise, being able to recognize how someone else makes a difference, and being able to figure out how to express it, takes time for quiet reflection that stereos and headsets don't provide.

Life calls us to continue growing. Besides needing to tell others, "thanks," and, "you're neat," we may want to begin telling them some specific examples. When I think about the people, both adults and teens, who seem special to me, these kinds of words come to mind: gentle, playful, energetic, positive, serious, open, willing to be vulnerable, helpful, outgoing, perceptive, humorous, kind, good at listening, honest, able to be trusted, patient, forgiving, generous, and loyal.

Each time I take the risk to be specific in my positive comments to others, I sense their appreciation. Sometimes they're surprised. Sometimes they say, "Do you really think so? No one has ever told me that before." Sometimes they look pleased or embarrassed. Regardless of their initial reaction, a number of people have told me some time later that my comments were useful, they thought about them frequently, and it helped them get through tough times when they were filled with self-doubt.

When I reflect on how greatly I've been influenced by other people's positive perceptions of me, and when I think of the lady who died so suddenly with no last chance to say those things she might have been saving up for the right time, it renews my determination to let people know the things I appreciate about them.

It takes a little practice to learn to be specific, but the end result is so rewarding: people who know clearly the ways in which they are pleasing and make a difference. It's worth the effort to learn how to let people know they matter.

CHAPTER FORTY TWO

ROBIN AND DAN

I t was an outdoor wedding, the binding of the lives and hopes of Dan and Robin. Balloons were everywhere, and masses of garden flowers were blooming at the home of Robin's parents. Robin's mother had smiled and wiped away tears of happy memories while working the garden into a showcase for her daughter's wedding.

Robin's father had built the decking and platform for the ceremony. He had used his design and building skills to construct a beautiful, gracious setting that housed the many different plots of flowers.

The place was rich with relatives who had journeyed thousands of miles, because major events were celebrated joyously by this family, no matter the inconvenience. Pride, warmth, and finishing touches were put on the house. Incomplete light fixtures gone begging for years were finally hung.

A cameraman stood on a platform near the place for the exchange of vows. One soon realized he had cerebral palsy by the sharp angle to the lean of his upper body, random contractions of his arms and fingers, and the occasional arch to his neck. He was an honored friend, working with his jacket off to videotape the crowd and ceremony. Using the ability of fingers that still took precise commands, he was crafting a present for the couple that would mirror their joy.

There was a gentleness and intimacy about the wedding, a sense of deep hospitality made real by the home setting, but one that would have been duplicated in a church because of the graciousness of the people involved.

It was a celebration, not of sophistication and splendor, but rather of friendships, families, and love; a love united and hopeful, inclusive and accepting, that sees beyond the surface of people to the qualities within.

The groom's parents had both died, and their presence was symbolized by a vase of roses given out later in the service. The groom's sister and brother-in-law walked him forward to the altar, but only after Dan had gently and lovingly walked with his retarded adult brother down the center aisle.

Dan and his brother were both dressed in white tuxes, and they walked slowly, allowing for the brother's shuffle and hesitancy in front of the crowd. Dan talked quietly to him as they walked in, easing his brother's discomfort, helping him catch the sacredness of the moment, and letting him know the joy they had that he was a part of their wedding.

Robin's gown had been caringly designed and sewn by a friend skilled in costume design. He had cherished the opportunity to show his affection for Dan and Robin in such a concrete way.The bridesmaids wore simple dresses of linen and lace; the groomsmen walked with them to the front, increasing the feeling that this was not to be a spectacle, but a gathering of friends.

People wiped tears from their eyes at the obvious emotion of the groom and the moments when the bride's voice broke during her vows. The radiance of the couple rekindled the memory of love dwelling in people; not the momentary love for the good times, but the enduring love that knows pain and disappointment and still trusts in a future together.

As part of the simple and personal religious service, the families of the bride and groom freed Dan and Robin to love each other's family. Then everyone at the wedding stood as a group and pledged their support to the new couple. Everything about the ceremony and festivities that followed said people were wonderful and worth investing in, that life could be full and good even while being flawed and painful.

The day was a statement that love could be not only intense and dramatic but more often slow, steady, and found after much time, effort and dedication. It was living testimony that love is given to us to give to one another.

CHAPTER FORTY THREE

VULNERABLE TO PAIN

L ove is a subtle thing, capable of sneaking up and leaving you feeling vulnerable and defenseless. For me, there's a unique poignancy that comes with loving teenagers.

There they are with all their bravado or defensiveness, giggling or awkwardness, roughhousing or shyness. They have assorted sizes and temperaments, abilities and prejudices, truths and attachments. As a group, they're initially just faces and names you try to connect.

Then somewhere, over time, it becomes unnecessary to think what name belongs with what kid. More is known about the individual, their humor, possibly a fear or two, some of their successes, the things other people like about them. There are kids who give a bit more, ones who will listen hard while they look like they're ignoring you, and ones who like more distance while still wanting to be a part of the whole.

You may begin thinking about them, not just the hour or two before being with them, but when their names appear in the paper, when thinking about the richness of your life, or when wrestling with fears about what it must be like to grow up today.

Then one day you recognize how much those kids have grown. You see added confidence, tenderness, a willingness to risk, a greater patience with others, or a deepened intensity about life. You swell with pride at their progress, are in awe of their maturity, and know for certain you're attached.

Being attached brings a sense of fullness with it. You feel a freshness inside when catching a smile and a wave, an inner expansion when sharing some teasing and good humored ribbing. You begin to wonder why some people don't like teens, and expect that you'll enjoy all teenage kids because the ones you know have become so special.

Then something invariably happens. Maybe it's a death of someone they knew, the death of a dream, a moment of painful exposure, a time of deep confusion, or the end of something special. At a time when you see their pain, you realize what happens to them matters greatly to you.

One moment you're mad at them, and you think, "What's the big deal, they're just kids. What difference could they mean to me?" Then you become more upset for awhile because you realize that no matter what they are, you love them, and when they hurt, you hurt. You feel powerless and vulnerable in the face of that kind of love.

Then again, they may see a moment of pain in your life and reach out as you did to them. Their attempts may be a bit more hesitant and unique, but you know the love you feel for them is mutual. They are invested in you, and your pain is also theirs.

Though you want to reassure them everything will be alright and the hurt will only last awhile, the truth is that life will often be harsh; love often brings pain. It's not easy to get involved with kids. You want to tell them all the painful things to avoid in the years ahead.

Then you begin to settle down, reflecting again on the richness and joy they offer, the sacredness of being allowed glimpses of their coming to maturity. You forget the intensity of the pain that can come with loving them. You look forward to being together again and sharing a part of your journey with such worthwhile companions.

CHAPTER FORTY FOUR

FIREPLACE PICNICS

"Fireplace picnics" started when our youngest was still needing naps and our oldest was showing signs of becoming the "family organizer."

The menu was always the same; to have varied it would have been to alter a tradition. Each item was essential; the event would have been incomplete without the presence of hot dogs and buns, onions and sauerkraut, ketchup and mustard, corn chips and orange drink, and the graham crackers, marshmallows and hershey bars destined to become s'mores.

Our event was much like any other family picnic except it was held indoors. Jim was responsible for building the fire; the kids helped. Twigs were gathered from the backyard pile, kindling from the barrel near the wood pile. Finally hardwood logs were chosen to assure the kind of coals necessary to roast marshmallows to golden perfection.

Just after the fire was laid came the laying of the "oil cloth", a piece of plastic-coated fabric, eight feet by ten feet. At one time it had hidden our furnace from view, making a basement bathroom out of a furnace room. We had learned after one try at "fireplace picnic" that the key to its success depended on not having to worry about spots or spills or typical picnic disasters.

A plastic tablecloth was simply not large enough to provide a working area for five, so we searched through packed-away belongings to find something that would work. We tried a painter's plastic drop-cloth, but it was too light weight for our active kids. Philip had poked holes in it with his toes as he jiggled around waiting for his turn with the hot dog stick.

Once furniture was pushed back against the wall, kids laid the cloth while I filled bowls with food. When we were new at fireplace picnics, we left hot dogs in the package. But juice leaked out onto the cloth, soaking our socks, so we learned to put the hot dogs in bowls. That meant another job for one of the kids, because our dog Smokey would try to help himself to whatever was unguarded. The onions and sauerkraut, however, were never threatened.

When the kids were very young, we had a rule of only two cooking at a time. But as years progressed, it was fun, and no longer life-threatening, for all of us to be huddled around the fire, joking, teasing and watching the progress of the food. With the passage of time, "brats" were added to help satisfy growing appetites, but everything else remained the same.

Also with the passage of time, relaxed conversation and moments of quiet staring into the fire became more common. Our fireplace picnics took on a richer dimension, growing from times of frantic excitement to ones of comfortable companionship.

Once when we were telling someone about our picnics, the person reacted with shock. "Don't you know how dangerous that is," she exclaimed. "The grease from the hot dogs will coat the surface of the chimney. Brats are even worse. You wait and see. You'll end up having a chimney fire that could burn your house down."

I was stunned. I wanted to totally disregard what she said, but she was a practical woman. She was usually right about things and full of common sense. I wanted to act responsibly, and I certainly didn't want our house to burn down or fill with smoke. But the thought of giving up our fireplace picnics was disturbing.

When I told Jim, he just shrugged his shoulders, his way of saying, "I don't think it's a big deal." But I still wondered. I figured we could clean the chimney each year, though I knew we probably wouldn't; we could cut down on the number of picnics, though I knew we probably wouldn't; or I could worry about it for awhile, which I did.

For several months, before and after the picnics, I would have some periods of doubt and concern. Were we really being careless? Were we letting our own pleasure get in the way of the responsible thing to do? I'd settle into bed the night of one of our picnics, still warm and happy from the glow of the fire and the enjoyment of the family; then the doubts would return.

One day, perturbed with the unsettled feeling I had, I sat myself down and said, "Look, Pat, life has risks and they're not all interpersonal. Do you or do you not want the picnics? If you do, minimize the risks and be done with it. What you're doing right now is nibbling away at your enjoyment and peace of mind by not resolving the situation. That's as irresponsible as opening yourself up to the risk of fire if it actually does exist."

The picnics were important to all of us, involving far more than filling our stomachs. The picnics were clearly quality time with our kids and with each other, times when moments of laughter, conflict, or learning allowed us to sense that we were "family." They had become times of "remember when" that gave each child a time in the limelight.

Possibly our practical friend hadn't experienced that kind of picnic or didn't believe that enjoyment was a good enough reason to take some risks, but I already knew that memories often need to be created and that good memories were reasons enough to take some risks.

The fireplace got cleaned, the picnics continued, and I resolved to let the issue of our fireplace picnics serve as a lesson to me about not letting the fear of practical risks nibble away at my life's enjoyment.

Learning to do that has been sweeter to me than our finest golden marshmallows, plump soft from the glowing embers. It's been a gift to myself as cherished as the first s'more given in love by a child flushed with effort and success.

CHAPTER FORTY FIVE

THE CERTAINTY OF SEASONS

In the eye of my mind I can still see Nana, shoulders slumped, hands in her apron pockets, staring out the window, slowly shaking her head from side to side.

"It's another gloomy day," she'd say, sighing deeply. "I feel so much happier when the sun shines." How many times did I hear that as a child, spending weekends with my dad's mother. She was a widow who doted over me, the only girl born into the family in seventy-three years.

She had time on her hands and looked forward to our weekends together. She would plan fun things for us to do like riding the street car to the zoo, or afternoon movies followed by sumptuous root-beer floats once we got home. We played old maid and slapjack by the hour and watched wrestling on her new TV. She wasn't above cheating at canasta if she thought she wouldn't be discovered.

Very few things dampened Nana's spirits, but gloomy, sunless days, especially several in a row, would put her into a mild depression. She seemed to lose interest even in doing her loved crocheting. She had less energy, less joy in living.

Years after her death, I read: "I believe in the sun even when it isn't shining; I believe in love even when there's no one there; and I believe in God even when He is silent." I thought of Nana because she seemed to lack that ability to get beyond the gloominess, to see beyond the immediate.

I feel like I've inherited Nana's sensitivity to sunless days. I find myself wondering whether it's inborn or whether I learned to respond that way from the many days I spent with her, watching how she related to the world. Then I laugh, because regardless of how much time I spend wondering, the fact remains that I'm affected by weather, sometimes at inconvenient times.

One spring I visited with a friend while she ordered incredible amounts of flower seeds and bulbs from an assortment of garden catalogs. She and her husband had moved to suburban Chicago, and they had a magnificent yard. I was so inspired that I, too, ordered seeds with dreams of a breath-taking yield.

But it was a miserable spring; it rained for forty days and forty nights. With each passing day, my soul shriveled a bit more and doubts about myself and others began to grow and flourish. My dreams for the garden became fears I could not set aside, and I never planted the flower seeds for fear that nothing would grow.

Strings of sunless days in other seasons have halted plans of various magnitude. For years I berated myself about not having the will power or determination to rise above the way I felt. Then I defended myself for years by saying it was wrong to deny my feelings. Fortunately, over those years I also learned about feelings being neither right nor wrong and about the ability to "act as if."

It's not wrong for me to feel gloomy on a sunless day, even if my husband moves along totally unaffected by the weather outside. His attitude is that he's certainly not going to let himself be affected by something he has no control over. As much as I admire that response, it's not how I feel and I've had to tell myself repeatedly it doesn't make him right and me wrong or him good and me bad.

Whereas I used to chastise myself about feeling low, now when I'm feeling the blues coming from too many sunless days or other sources, I tell myself I'm only feeling a feeling. It was so much easier to get into "shame -on-me" for feeling down when I focused on what the feeling was; it seems to diffuse that whole shame business much better to simply say I'm feeling a feeling.

Part of that undoubtedly stems from labeling certain feelings as negative or bad. Hardly anyone experiences much discomfort from admitting to themselves or someone else they are feeling joy, gratitude, affection, happiness, or elation. But few people could say the same thing about anger, jealousy, rage, sadness, or self-pity. Yet, feelings are feelings. And even though negative feelings are important to recognize and often prompt actions that may or may not be healthy and just, they're no more right or wrong than positive ones.

Remembering to say, "I'm feeling a feeling," helps me when I begin to judge myself harshly for what I'm feeling. "Acting as if" is the second tool to help me get on with my life when things become more than I feel I can handle.

Sometimes I feel unloved or unappreciated. Sometimes I feel like I'm being judged harshly by other people; like I never really do a job the way it should be done, or that I'm the only one who can't "get it together." What I know in my head – that those things are only rarely true – is not what I tell myself. That's when I have to acknowledge what I'm feeling and go on to act as if I were loved and appreciated, accepted by others, doing an adequate job, and "had it together."

Rather than deny feelings and find unhealthy ways to comfort myself, I try to acknowledge them and act as if things were otherwise. This allows me freedom to have my feelings catch up with my actions as I proceed in more confident, self-accepting ways.

Are there times when that doesn't work, when accepting my feelings without judgement and "acting-as-if" doesn't relieve my being psychologically down? Being honest, I have to say yes. What then?

Over the years I've come to know there are seasons of the soul just as surely as there are seasons of nature. Every promise of spring, every warmth and fullness of summer, every dwindling and slowing of fall, and every desolate moment of winter has found a parallel in my soul, a parallel as fully wonderful or frightening as what creation offers.

The playing of the seasons, time and time again, has produced its memories and given me strong images on which to rely. As surely as spring follows winter and summer precedes fall, there will be the unfolding of seasons in my life bringing joy or pain. During those seasons of trial, when my best efforts to understand and manage the pain no longer work, I need to hold fast to the truth that no season is forever. Even the harshest interval has its limit, and patience and hope make sense.

It's happened again and again. The change of seasons in nature and in my soul has resulted in a wisdom I choose to trust.

CHAPTER FORTY SIX

THE GIFT OF HER SMILE

S he worked hard at her smile, first for herself and then for others. I remember our meeting as if it were yesterday, though I think it was possibly nineteen years ago. We were at a meeting and asked to do some kind of small group exercise when I first noticed her.

We had been asked to speak for one minute about ourselves without saying anything negative, and we were all nervous and awkward, laughing a bit and trying to squeeze in a few more minutes of small talk. We'd introduced ourselves, but were all anxious enough so that we were pretty much thinking only about ourselves, wondering if we'd survive the day.

What caught my attention was her smile. It was radiant and when she turned her full attention on me, smile included, I felt personally noticed and enjoyed by her. It occurred to me that she probably wasn't what many people would consider an attractive woman in the classic sense of the word. She wouldn't have been one of the first noticed in a roomful of women.

But oh, her smile...it was so wonderful and full. Once you really noticed it and felt it, you had to say something. Our small group process included a feedback exercise, and so I told her what a beautiful smile she had.

She said that she joined the speech club in high

school thinking it would help her shyness. She knew she was what people considered plain, so she felt she needed something extra to help her gain confidence and give her speeches an added advantage. She concentrated her efforts on finding a smile that would please herself and others.

She experimented in front of the mirror as only an early adolescent can, trying dozens of styles and poses until she found the one she thought would bring the most enjoyment to others. Then she began to practice, with effort and humor, perfecting a smile that made others feel noticed and special. It was a gift she developed to its fullest.

What seemed so special to me about this woman was that she didn't seem to have developed her smile for herself, although that might have been her original intent. She developed her smile for others, not to make people think she was more attractive but rather to make others feel more attractive.

Developing a smile probably isn't seen by many as a grand accomplishment. It didn't make money, change social policy or effect a cure. It probably wasn't even an award-winning smile. But with her smile alone, she brightened my day, made me feel noticed and special, and helped me forget for a few moments some of life's grim realities.

She made me want to learn to smile, to do for others what she had done for me. That in itself was a gift.

CHAPTER FORTY SEVEN

IT'S THE
REAL THING

Living in Owatonna means being exposed to an abundance of artists and performers, including Jim Killen, the renowned wildlife artist. Many times I've been in a group of people admiring a print when someone has said, "It's a Killen," in a tone of voice that says, "and that means it's special." No one could argue with that.

One of Jim's prints is of an enormous moose standing alone in a field during a snowstorm. Over the course of a couple years, I'd admired the print in a number of places. Then one day I happened to be in the Killen home and saw the moose painting. I think it might have been hanging above a fireplace, but the impact of seeing it was so great that I'm really not sure where in the house it hung. I just know that when I saw it I instinctively knew it was the real thing, the painting from which all of the moose prints had originated.

The painting was pure, clean, large, and powerful. I don't know enough artist's terms to discuss it well. I do know that it stopped me in my tracks with the feeling that raises hair, and a part of me said, "There is something so right about that, and I want it."

Life has those kinds of moments, too; moments that are so human or so right we know instinctively they're the way life was meant to be. There was a high school junior who put that kind of label on a camping experience he was describing to a group during an informational and fund-raising evening for our local Young Life organization.

I'd been a counselor at the camp a couple summers before, so I'd experienced first hand (and then some) what Pete had learned. First of all, camp was high energy. It was the kind of high energy created by bringing together a couple hundred kids, from diverse areas and backgrounds, determined to have the time of their lives.

Secondly, it was high fun parasailing, surf-jetting, waterskiing, running relays, playing challenge games, singing, and watching crazy skits. It involved high cooperation for group-building challenges in which no one succeeded unless the group worked together as a whole. The strongest got that way only by helping the weakest to succeed.

High trust was won over time by honest, open discussion about things that mattered in life; discussions between kids and between adults and kids. There was high meaning in learning about Jesus Christ and the meaning he could have in one's life. There was high support in hugs and tender touches, arms around shoulders, a willingness to be vulnerable, a caring and sharing that was appropriate, special, and very good.

Often during our stay at camp someone would talk about what it was going to be like when we got back into the real world. We knew that what we experienced was in a controlled environment intended to produce the very things that made it so special.

What Pete said about camp at the banquet is this, "I learned that this time at camp was the real world..." It was the real thing – the stop you in your tracks, raise your hair, real thing.

And isn't it so? When you're loved, really loved unconditionally for who you are, do you ever truly forget or doubt it? When you are really trusted with someone's fears or shame or doubts; when someone allows themselves to be unglamorous, unmanly or vulnerable in your presence, do you ever really forget it?

When you're allowed to be tender and caring, free from suspicion of motives and "where's-this-going?"; when you're allowed to be friends with a friendship built on honesty, respect and mutual enjoyment, doesn't the memory of that linger forever? When you're entrusted with someone's spiritual insights, offered a chance to view another's journey toward truth about life, don't you feel humbled and grateful?

Pete said it, "That's the real world. That's the way life is intended to be." Tell me that wisdom isn't found in seventeen-year-olds, and I'll introduce you to Pete to prove you wrong. Pete saw it, felt it, and lived it: life as it was intended to be. The real thing.

CHAPTER FORTY EIGHT

MATTERS
OF THE HEART

The sun was out today, bright and magnificent, reflecting off the snow. It filled me with a new-found energy after too many days of gray dreariness. A cluster of sunless days chips away at my spirit in ways that leave me frustrated at feeling so vulnerable to something as uncontrollable as weather. And yet it's true; I respond like a barometer to changes in sunlight. So when the warmth and magic of a blazing winter sun arrived today, I didn't waste a minute using the energy it provided.

A fair portion of that energy was spent cleaning out a room euphemistically known as the "computer room," to reflect the work done in it now, the "craft room" in memory of the months that it served as my workshop during a craft and stenciling business, or "Phil's old room" in honor of its past inhabitant.

It's a room I'm fond of whether spotless or trashed. It houses shelf upon shelf of books: old, new, reference, entertaining, religious, inspirational, classic, marginal, children's and adult's. It holds thousands of hours of enjoyment in four hundred books that represent memories of being curled up in someone else's adventures or sitting side by side with a child reading aloud.

There's also a wonderful desk in the room. It's a roll-top, pigeon-holed desk, an imitation of one that might have graced a colonial home. Sometimes that desk gets stacked taller than is safe, which usually means about shoulder high. Then it becomes time to sort and pitch. Full sunshine makes that a wonderful task, and so it was with pleasure that I settled into my cozy nest of stimulation to return the desk to its rightful dignity.

As I reached the writing surface, I discovered an article I wrote in April of our son's senior year in high school. Since Phil was now a college sophomore, I found it somewhat amusing to read, especially because it was filled with pain at the separation we faced with his leaving home.

It talked about how surprised Jim and I felt at the pain of our second child's leaving. We expected some pain when Ann left, our first encounter with a child leaving home. But we certainly hadn't expected to feel that way about the second child's leaving, having been veterans by then.

It doesn't happen that way, does it, becoming veterans in matters of the heart? Oh, there are a few things I've gotten more "used to," a few things repeated enough in my life so they don't immobilize me in ways they used to. I can now say goodbye to a friend leaving town without literally sobbing on the curb while their car pulls away, but mostly it's just the expression of pain that has changed.

Matters of the heart are always new. It was just as painful in the months before Philip's departure as it would have been if he were our first to leave home. While it was some small comfort reminding ourselves we had survived and grown beyond the pain of Ann's leaving, it didn't stop the feeling of pain. We wanted to extend and frame each precious moment we spent with Phil so we might be able to savor them during the times we would be apart.

As we look at our youngest daughter, less than eighteen months from following her longings to be more independent, we sometimes succumb to the temptation to pretend that her leaving won't be as painful. "We've now gone through it twice. How could we be more prepared? Besides, aren't we beginning to enjoy the additional time we have to ourselves to become 'a couple' again?"

And then for all our bravado, we discover that we're trying to create more time together with Monica at a time in her development when she is necessarily drawing away and preparing to strike out on her own. We catch ourselves sometimes disappointed that she's not eager to be with us. The reality of another child soon to leave home then becomes painful, and we need to be honest with ourselves about it.

Failing to be honest about something that is painful provides too great a temptation to medicate the pain away, distract the pain away by getting overly busy, or pretend the pain away by acting as if everything is fine. What's foolish about that is it also prevents the beginning of a grieving that will only be resolved in the experience of the pain. Postponing the moments of pain, or pushing them aside also prevents savoring wonderful memories.

Matters of the heart deserve full attention. That was the message of the column I wrote and rediscovered on my cluttered desktop. We have three children, each unique and special, and the comings and goings of their lives are times of joy and pain for us.

It's curious how reminders of our own wisdom can sometimes catch us off guard, and it's wonderful that such unlikely moments as sorting and dusting on a sun-filled day can bring us back in touch with the basics of life.

CHAPTER FORTY NINE

REASON
TO REJOICE

His name was Nelder and I met him at the local lumber company. At first he would do mostly paperwork at the desk behind the counter. Then one especially busy day he left the desk to wait on me. After that, he usually came to the counter to help when I came in.

I'd stand there on Saturday mornings with my list of materials and questions in hand, surrounded by building contractors, and Nelder would wait on me and give me as much of his time as I needed. While the contractors were buying lumber and supplies by the houseloads, I was discussing my plans for napkin holders that could serve as 4-H projects. Yet he treated me as if I had the biggest bankroll in the place.

Nelder's the one I went to after I bent two drill bits trying to sink holes for bookshelves into our cement block basement walls. I was determined to do some easy carpentry without Jim's assistance and was feeling a delightful pride in using the small power saw and drill, until I bent the two bits. Nelder introduced me to masonry bits and never once acted as if I should have left the job for Jim to do.

He's also the one I finally turned to in desperation after fusing my thumb to a tube of super glue—covering the instructions on how to avoid or repair such a disaster.

Other than saying, "You did what?," he didn't laugh about my situation. He just got a tube and solemnly read the directions over the phone. I knew from the smiles of the staff the next time I was in that Nelder had passed the word, but he spared me having to hear the story while I was there.

I'm not sure if it was months or years that I knew Nelder that way, always giving me as much time as I needed, always giving equal attention to our kids as they began to tackle building projects. He never said there was no such thing as a dumb question. He simply treated me in such a way that I never felt foolish about approaching him with my uncertainties.

For however long he waited on me, I still hadn't known his name or even how he fit into the hierarchy of jobs at the lumber yard. Then one Friday morning I was reading the newspaper and saw an invitation to join the Alexander Lumber staff in saying farewell to Nelder, who was retiring as manager of the lumber company. It was a coffee and cookie farewell to him and a welcoming in of the new manager.

The hours of the open house were for the most part passed, so I had only minutes to figure out how I was going to express my thanks to this gentle man who had been so helpful and reassuring to me as I developed confidence in new areas of my life.

I had a local florist blow up three balloons, and since it was before the days of balloons with messages, I had 'thank you' written on them with magic marker. In the meantime I wrote a quick note to Nelder telling him how much I appreciated the attention he gave me, what it meant to be treated with the same importance and consideration extended to their largest accounts.

When I walked into Alexander's, most of the people celebrating were already gone, and Nelder was sitting back at his desk behind the counter. He saw the balloons first, then me, and for a moment he looked confused. Then he noticed the thank you on the balloons and slowly began to get up from his desk, his eyes brimming with tears. He took my card, read it slowly, looked at me awhile and then gave me a gentle hug.

He said nothing, and I know he couldn't have without emotion breaking through in a way neither of us wanted or needed. In fact, Nelder never again made mention of my gesture of gratitude even on the occasional times that we'd run into each other downtown. He didn't need to. He had a way of saying with his eyes that I had touched him with my thanks in lasting ways.

That memory still sustains me and reminds me how we all rely on knowing we matter to one another. I had intended simply to say thanks to Nelder for the treatment I'd received, and instead I learned that who I was and how I expressed myself made a difference in someone's life. My gratitude and the effort that went into expressing it was rewarded a hundredfold.

Over the years I've come to know with certainty what I'd been taught as a child: that goodness is rewarded abundantly in this life, not simply in the next. As a child I hoped it was true, as an adult I've lived enough years to have seen it happen again and again. Granted, it hasn't always been immediate, a give and take situation. Sometimes it's taken years to actually see the return. But I know because I've experienced it that gratitude and generosity return to the giver, multiplied as surely and as evidently as Nelder's reaction on his retirement day.

That alone is reason to rejoice.

CHAPTER FIFTY

LOVE DOESN'T READ MINDS

What strange notions we allow ourselves to have about love. The temptation to romanticize love, to want it to be all-involving and all-encompassing, to expect it to make another person capable of knowing our needs, can produce harm beyond belief.

It may feel wonderful to cherish the belief that if others really loved us they would know what we wanted without our having to tell them. It's a heart-warming fantasy to dream that somewhere there's a person who will know our innermost wants because of their love for us. "He'll know what I'm thinking before I even say it."

I once knew a woman who wore embarrassingly cheap jewelry she presented as authentic. She would show it off and brag about it while the rest of us were either amused or saddened at her need to delude herself. In matters of love, it's not quite as easy to know when we're like the woman worshipping junk. But when we believe that if another person loved us enough we wouldn't have to tell them what we wanted, we're close .

Years ago I laid in the hospital as the staff tried valiantly to prevent the premature birth of our second child. It was a long process, well over fifteen hours before it ended in sadness. About three hours into the ordeal, Jim turned to me and said, "There's nothing more I can do here. I'll be at work if they need me," and left for his job that was only blocks away. "I can be here in just a few minutes if you need me," he told the nurses as he left.

I was shocked. "How can he leave me?," I thought. "Doesn't it even matter to him how I feel? What's so blessed important about his job that he can't take a few hours to be with me?" And with all the wisdom that one has after two years of marriage, I concluded that Jim didn't love me as much as I thought he did. It never occurred to me that he was having great difficulty feeling powerless in the face of impending death that had also robbed him of his parents while he was a young child.

I felt abandoned, and rather than say a simple, "Please stay. I need you with me," I embraced the pain and shock of feeling "unloved." I held them in a secret place in my heart for years, to take them out and look at when I was feeling sorry for myself.

Years later I talked with a woman who was having one-day surgery. "My husband's not even going to stay. He's dropping me off and going to work," she said with disgust.

"Have you told him you'd like him to stay?", I asked, remembering my story years back.

"If he doesn't know that by now, I'm sure not going to tell him," she complained. "Besides, he's so in love with that damn job he'd probably say 'no' anyway. He's never around when I need him."

I usually don't give advice but this time I did, and it had to do with taking the risk of asking her husband to stay with her, telling him she needed him close, that she needed to know he was in the hospital while she was in surgery.

"But if he really loved me he would know those things. I shouldn't have to tell him," she moaned again. "It doesn't mean as much if I have to ask for it. It feels like begging.

He should know how I feel and want to be there because he loves me," she cried as I began to talk about hidden expectations and the unfairness of expecting others to know our wants and needs.

It's garbage to assume people will know our wishes because of loving us. Granted, over time, a husband, friend, parent or sibling will come to know certain things about us. There may be certain things we enjoy, or that person may enjoy surprising us with little tokens and moments of caring. They may be the type, over time, who sense our unspoken moods and respond as they know we would wish. But love doesn't bring with it the ability to read minds, and untold damage is done to relationships when we allow ourselves to believe that people who love us should know what we are thinking or feeling.

The danger with such nonsense is that we begin to hold hidden agendas, a list of something we want or expect will happen. Then we judge the good intentions of others and the quality of their love for us based on the things we have kept secret.

I think of a woman who always made birthdays a special event. She was in a group of women who, because of their busy schedules, began setting aside one day each month to celebrate birthdays. Yet she was heartsick that only one friend had sent her a card on her actual birthday, rather than waiting until the day of "the party." What a simple matter it could have been to be able to playfully or directly let her friends know she would prefer to get her cards on her "very own day."

Another women, close to my age, amazed me when she said she'd learned in the first year of her marriage to state her wishes clearly. She said it just wasn't worth all the misery of expecting her husband to know what she wanted and then being disappointed when he didn't. The amazing thing was that she wasn't talking about gifts, she was talking about needs in their relationship, hopes that she had about how they spent time together or about the kind of attention and affirmation she knew she needed.

That kind of openness takes work. But more importantly, it requires giving up a seductively dangerous, false notion of love that we cling to because it seems so wonderful. Taking charge of expressing our needs to those we love means giving up the childhood dream that someone will love us without cost and answer our needs out of the magic of romance.

Of course the other risk, the greater risk than giving up a childhood fantasy, is that once we have expressed our needs or wants, we remain terribly vulnerable because the other person may be unable or unwilling to meet our request. Maybe the quality of the relationship would be found lacking, or maybe a person would have to stop expecting someone else to meet their every need.

Those are real risks that frighten people and keep them from speaking their needs. It's easier, "lovelier," to pretend that love can read minds. Well, it can't, and we do a disservice to ourselves and others every time we fall into the trap of thinking it can. Love is hard, often wonderful work that flourishes when people speak the needs of their hearts clearly enough so others can respond in love. Let's give real love a chance.

CHAPTER FIFTY ONE

GESTURES OF LOVE

To be around Chuck is to be around dynamic, fun-filled, serious energy. Chuck is a Young Life director. He makes his living and finds his purpose connecting with teens and funneling his energy into activities they enjoy.

Chuck shares the depth of the Gospel, as he understands it in his life, with the same ease with which he plays basketball or guitar at group meetings. Kids listen because what Chuck says rings true, and most kids are hungry to hear what credible adults believe.

Besides getting to know Chuck, kids got to know his wife and children and learn what went on in their family life. So it was common for them to know Chuck was going to run in his first mini-triathalon. They knew he began his training late but was determined to see it through.

Chuck made a decent showing in the triathalon, better than a number of the kids he'd known through Young Life Club and time spent at the high school, and a healthy amount of good-natured ribbing resulted.

Then Chuck ran a second time, out of state, in a seven-miler. The weather was hot and humid, and suddenly this larger-than-life man was collapsed on the pavement. He was taken to the first aid tent and sent by ambulance to the hospital's intensive care unit.

Messages came by phone; they were sketchy, imprecise, and scary. They contained words like collapse, heart attack, and critical time. We were numb. We knew things like that happened, but not to thirty-five year olds, at least not to Chuck.

More messages came. They sounded better and more hopeful. We learned quickly about exercise-induced asthma attacks and the pneumonia resulting from breathing in vomit at the time of collapse. We also learned of the frightening things that had to be ruled out in the process of coming to that diagnosis.

We kept thinking of Chuck's wife, of what it must have been like for Bonnie to be waiting at the finish line growing ever more concerned, and what it must have been like later for his kids to see him on the respirator. Kyle and Mandy are young, but old enough to know when something is serious and unexpected. They know enough about death to know it happens, even to dads.

When Chuck returned from the hospital after four days, he was still fatigued. This was a Chuck no one had ever experienced before, a Chuck easily winded and exhausted by the simplest act of walking around inside the house. It was hard to believe he could do so little. After having come to expect such high energy from Chuck, it was also frustrating for everyone.

His endurance gradually increased, but it was common for Chuck to suffer brief setbacks. In an effort to see what he could tolerate, he would occasionally overdo. When those times came, there was nothing more to be done than for Chuck to catch a nap to allow his energy to rebuild.

One of these setbacks was particularly strong, and Chuck all but dragged himself to bed at mid-afternoon. He was fearful he wouldn't be able to get the rest he needed with his three children home, and he felt guilty that Bonnie would once again have to try to keep things quiet. When five year old Kyle came bounding into the bedroom, Chuck was even more concerned that if he didn't get his needed rest, something worse might occur.

"Whatcha doing, Dad, taking a nap?" bellowed Kyle in his usual big voice. "Can I sleep with you?" Chuck was tempted to pretend he was already dozing, to not respond hoping Kyle might quickly assess the situation as boring and move on. But at the same time, Chuck remembered those hours in the hospital, his thoughts while on the respirator, and his realizations of the preciousness of life and family.

"Kyle, I'm really, really tired and I have to take a rest. Okay?," Chuck said, hoping he wouldn't also have to ask Kyle to leave, but knowing there wasn't room for a compromise.

By that time Kyle had crawled onto the bed. "I'll sleep with you, Dad," said the lad who had given up naps two years before. Moments of silence passed. Chuck lay on his side facing Kyle, who had curled up beside him. Then in a quiet that was carefully preserved, Chuck felt a blanket being gently, protectively pulled up to cover him and a tender kiss on his right elbow.

Finally, in a gesture born out of a desire to be near and comfort the dad he adored, Kyle placed his cheek on the back of Chuck's outstretched hand and promptly fell asleep.

That desire to be near and comfort lies deep within us. It was already well formed in five year old Kyle. Few of us will have opportunities as dramatic as intensive care units and respirators to prompt us to respond unafraid to the frailty or pain of others. But all of us will have times when being truly human will mean reaching out gently and protectively to someone in need.

When that time comes, remember Kyle: a small boy; a small gesture; a grand moment.

CHAPTER FIFTY TWO

FLOWERS IN THE RAINFALL

I t amazes me at times to discover I'm pondering things stored in the far recess of my memory years after the fact. Lying in bed one Sunday morning, having been awakened by the early rays of dawn, I was coaxing a chapter or two from a book. I was half way between sleep and wakening, when words from a song in the sixties tumbled into my thoughts, no doubt prompted by something I'd read.

> *"So, I'll continue to continue to pretend my life will never end,*
> *And flowers never bend in the rainfall."*

When I was learning that song years ago, it was a song with a pleasing melody, possibly by Simon and Garfunkel, with guitar chords I could play. I'm sure the words must have said something to me then, because I remember playing it often. But the wisdom of those words remembered on that early Sunday morning, struck me with a force as never before.

Over the years I've put together a perennial garden of plants I've begged, borrowed and stolen from willing, generous people who needed to thin out their gardens or wanted to share a treasure with me. I struggled to create a yard that suited the needs of a young, active family.

I lacked both the resources and discipline to purchase and plant flowers each year. I also lacked knowledge about what to plant when and why. I knew only that some flowers come up year after year to "do their thing" with little demand on their grateful beholder. Those were the kind of plants I needed, and in the years that followed, I carved more and more garden space out of a lawn that tried annually to reclaim its rightful space.

During those first seasons of digging and arranging, interrupted by all the necessary duties of a young mother, I came to know some of the personalities and temperaments of the flowers. But as yet they held no lessons of life for me. Weeding the garden was a peaceful break from my usual routine, and I enjoyed getting my hands dirty, smelling the pungency of the soil, and feeling sore tightened muscles after hours in the garden.

The seasons spent there made me feel more "country." I'd grown up a city kid whose mother tended the flower beds without my help. Because our first home had few flowers, my planting and tending was confined to indoor plants.

When we moved to a rural community, I was affected by the surrounding farms. Living in a city that relied on the farmer for its vitality, I experienced the draw of the land. More time spent outdoors coaxing life from the earth felt natural, and I was grateful for these new experiences.

Then I discovered that rabbits were going to challenge me for the right to enjoy my tulips, slugs were going to slime around whether I liked it or not, and iris boarers would concern a number of neighbors until the county extension agent identified them. I learned that weeds would grow overnight, lawns truly can reclaim stolen flower beds, and neglect would cost dearly.

I learned that young sons with power mowers barely under control could change the contour of a garden in minutes, and that ballgames, tag and dogs digging for buried fish could work faster than I at rearranging things.

But mostly I learned that perennials do come up with wonderful regularity, in spite of my most blatant neglect, and that I would be the delighted beholder of far more beauty than I had ever worked for.

Years have passed, and I don't garden as much now. But the lessons eked from garden soil seem to speak much more to life today than they did when I was learning where to place the crocuses and daffodils.

Like the chorus of the song mentioned, it's an illusion that flowers never bend in the rainfall. I remember storms that literally flattened our bed of narcissus, pounded them to the ground, and muddied them beyond my hopes of repair. The first such storm, which delighted me with its fury before I realized what it could do to flowers, sent me back into the house in tears after I surveyed the garden.

"All that work and all that beauty," I cried, "it's not fair." But the next morning dawned bright, clear, and crisp, and I found the flowers still a bit soiled, but clearly at half-mast, showing every sign of returning to full strength.

And that is life; not the illusion that "flowers never bend in the rainfall," but the reality that there are often storms in life that seem to flatten a soul beyond recovery. Only later do we recognize that, over time, the strength to survive has bolstered a person to stand tall again, fully vulnerable to the next downpour.

How else could it be? Much of life is simply beyond our control, even with the best of care and attention. Oh, it's true there are things I can do to help condition my flowers, care I can give them to help maximize their strength and endurance. They're healthier in soil that's fertilized, weed-free, and treated to help prevent invasion by pests or animals. They survive better when they're at full health.

So do people. There are things each one of us need to do for ourselves to help condition our lives for unavoidable onslaught. Each of us, over the years, is responsible for learning what those things are. For some it's being close to family or friends; for some, it's solitude; some need a relationship with their God; and others require a combination of all these things. We differ in our chosen supports.

Yet whatever our strength, in the rage of the storm when the fury is unrelenting, even the best defended will feel terror or pain and be stricken. It's at this time we need to remember that flowers do bend in the rainfall, and sometimes they flatten. But they also recover to stand tall and beautiful again.

CHAPTER FIFTY THREE

SIDE BY SIDE

They sat side by side in the sun, he facing in because the sunlight was too bright for his old eyes, she facing out because she revelled at the feel of spring sunshine on her face. They were in his room, and even though it was in a nursing home and occupied by another man as well, they always thought of it as his room.

He had been there for over a year now, almost fifteen months, and their daily visits were like gold to both of them. He was the grandfather, eighty-six and growing frail. She was the granddaughter, thirty-five and in her prime. Each day she listened to the same stories: stories of his youth, sleigh rides, horse and buggy days, barn dances and tent revivals. She heard about how he met her grandmother, how she'd been someone else's wife until death widowed her at thirty-one.

She wondered at what it meant for him to have left behind his rose gardens and workshop with not a word of regret, to leave behind children and grandchildren and come to a strange town, satisfied to be near her. For a long time she thought it had to do with the kind of man he was. Only recently had she begun to realize that it had to do with her healing from the death of her father.

They loved each other in a way that was beyond their disappointments and failures, and they enjoyed the freedom of not having to worry about what the other one thought. So it wasn't startling when he began to talk about dying, even though he seemed in good, though frail health.

He said, "I'd like to see your mother again before I die," and then was silent.

She wasn't sure what to say. She had read some Kubler-Ross and so knew a bit about death and dying. She also knew that a little bit of knowledge could be a dangerous thing. But they loved each other, and this was the first time he had talked about dying.

"I'll miss you when you're gone, but we'll be okay if you go," she said, adding, "It's been a privilege to get to know you as I have."

"I love you," he replied, "You have the biggest heart of anyone I know."

"I would have been proud to have you as a father or a husband," she returned.

"I loved your mother as if she were my flesh and blood," came his response. "I never wanted my own children after marrying your grandmother. Your mother and her sister were enough for me."

Then she thanked him for all the ways he had made her feel so special. He thanked her in the same way, and their tears began to slowly fall. They talked about the other members in her family, her husband and children, and the good times they had.

Then she said, "Think of all the people who will be there to greet you when you get to the other side," because he had often talked about all his friends in heaven as being on "the other side." But this time her words seemed painful, and he reacted with a fear she'd never seen.

"You believe that, don't you," she asked, amazed.

"Yes," he said, with a fear more visible, "but what if it isn't true?"

She realized then with a shock that even the strongest faith must confront moments of doubt in the face of death. It drove fear deep into her core and she prayed she'd be spared the test.

They talked a while longer. Then she left and went home to call her mother. "Gramp is talking about dying," she told her mother over the phone, "and he's never done that before. I think you should come."

"You know I'm coming," her mother reminded. "I'll be down on Saturday just as we planned. I've got a garage full of geraniums to plant, and I can't let them go until after Mother's Day."

"You do what you want," her daughter continued impatiently. "I just know Saturday is two days away, and I wouldn't wait that long if I were you."

"But his health has been stable..."

"He's talking about dying," the daughter persisted.

The mother called back again shortly after dawn the next morning. "I found someone to tend my geraniums. I'll be down in three hours."

The granddaughter was in the grandfather's room when her mother arrived. "It's so good to see you one last time before I die," he said, and the granddaughter left shortly after so the two of them could be alone.

They visited again on Saturday and others visited on Sunday. He died Monday morning in his wheelchair, watching from the doorway for his granddaughter to come off the elevator. She feared he had realized he was dying and tried to get to her. If she hadn't stopped to visit after a meeting, she thought, she could have been with him when he died.

But the nurses assured her he had a good morning and that he was sitting in the doorway, smiling and joking with the staff when death came swiftly and mercifully. In spite of her pain, the granddaughter knew this was so, and she was grateful.

She walked over to his chair and sat for awhile in the sunshine. Slowly she pulled the petals from a tulip and remembered their gentle goodbyes. The words, "Life is hello, life is goodbye," came to her. She knew they'd been a part of both, and she was ready to let go.

CHAPTER FIFTY FOUR

DETERMINED
TO BE WHOLE

I knew when I saw all the cars pulled to the side of the road, the people walking, the cameras and tripods and binoculars, that we weren't just bird-watching. It was also evident that most of us knew little about the birds drawing all the attention.

"That's the female isn't it?"

"No, I heard it's the baby about ready to leave the nest."

"Really? I don't think so." And on and on went the exchanges of conversation. Three, four, then six people joined in, looking upward all the while at a sixty-foot white pine just off the roadway.

A pair of Bald Eagles, an endangered species usually shy of crowds and preferring a wilderness habitat, had built their characteristically huge nest in full view of Highway 6 near Crosslake, Minnesota. It was completely visible to even the most casual passerby.

The rarity of the sight and numerous Fourth of July holiday travellers combined to produce a non-stop stream viewers. Dozens of folks stopped between sunup and sundown to stand, gaze, chat, exclaim and invariably fall silent at the strength and courage of the eagles, and the realization that they had chosen to continue life despite the encroachment on their habitat.

The enormity of the nest and equally incredible size of the eaglet captured imaginations. People stayed longer and felt the spirit within us all that continues to try against all odds.

Staring at the unbelievable nest of branches, grass, and other scavenged articles and at all the people drawn to it, I thought back to another time, four years before. I was headed to Rocky Mountain National Park to go camping with our son Philip. We were excited about the trip, energized by most everything we saw that looked different from Minnesota.

As we drove northwest from Denver, we noticed more and more bicyclers, young and old men and women pushing themselves to keep pace as they pedaled up mountain foothills at elevations that tested even the most experienced athlete. At first Phil and I talked about each biker that we passed: their age, style, or bike. We hadn't realized that we were in prime training ground for international bike racers and would see a steady stream of them even when we entered the steeper mountains.

After the first hour, however, the sight of bikers became so common that our thoughts and conversation turned once again to the camping trip. We soon began a particularly long ascent up a mountain grade and noticed a pack of bikers, possibly a dozen, working laboriously up the road. We grew silent in the face of such sheer effort, entertaining our own private thoughts about the determination required for such a strenuous ride.

Then we saw a biker who remains indelibly etched in our minds. His bike was lurching; we noticed that first and thought his wheel was loose. But he didn't pull to the side of the road as we expected; he kept on going, still lurching, but with a rhythm that made us realize that whatever the cause, it wasn't equipment failure.

By then our car had pulled alongside him, Phil and I still straining to figure out what was happening. What we saw was a young man, scarlet-faced with effort, sweating, straining, and throwing his weight into each revolution. He was missing one leg and lurching because the effort of pedaling his bike one-legged up the mountain meant having to throw his entire weight into staying upright.

We were stunned for a moment, and then our spirits soared. We honked the horn, threw him the thumbs up sign, tossed back our heads and said, "Yes!" He grinned in full appreciation of our admiration and support and kept on lurching determinedly up the mountain.

The eagles in Crosslake and the biker out of Denver both determined that life would have a place for them. They were willing to take a shot at the close to impossible because not to do so would be to settle for too much less.

How many times must that biker have fallen, his good leg held fast to the pedal by a foot strap? How many times did someone have to lift him up and take the bike off him so he could try again? Clearly we were seeing him after months of setbacks and defeat. But we were also seeing him alive and challenged with effort, and we felt a sense of kinship with him even though we wondered aloud if we'd be able to endure what he had.

We all have that spark in us, that tiny gift of determination to survive against the odds, to muster our energies and do the difficult rather than be diminished. I'm not sure what particular set of circumstances, what thoughts and determinations, put that one-legged young man back on his bike after such a cruel injury, but I do know that the same God that drove the biker from within is ready to drive each of us to wholeness if we want it.

The journey to wholeness can be exhilarating and energizing. It can also be frightening and exhausting, far more challenging than any of us were led to believe. But I have a saying on my mirror I know is true because it has happened in my life and continues to happen, just as surely as the eagles built their nest in Crosslake and the young man lurched up the mountain. It says:

> "To the extent that we search deeply into our inner self and recognize our own poverty, the Lord will give us the strength we need for an inner journey to wholeness."

WHEN
IS IT DAY?

I once heard someone described as having "the morals of an alley cat." I've never forgotten it, not because it shocked me or made me change my mind about the caring I had for that person, but because there's something so universal about the description.

At a certain level most of us struggle with having "the morals of an alley cat." Granted we may not show it in the same way this person did, with repeated short-term relationships of some intensity, but most of us struggle to fill a certain emptiness within us as we grow toward wholeness.

Maybe it's by overeating, freely gossiping, overspending, over consuming, or over possessing. Maybe it's by being over-dependent, under-committed, compulsively active or selfish.

Whatever the method, most of us are quite alike in trying to fill or divert ourselves enough so we don't have to face the incompleteness of our lives or our failure to meet the challenges of living justly. Until we look inward at our shadow self and recognize our alley cat, we will only be able to look outward and decry the alley cat in others.

In contrast, not long ago I had the privilege of being able to read a letter that was sent to a middle-aged woman by a young man in college. It was a beautiful, tender, appreciative letter that spoke freely of a relationship of respect and love. A mutual admiration existed between them.

Cynics would say, "What does a woman that age see in a kid his age?," or "Who's getting what out of that relationship?" Until we take the risk of true loving, we will not be able to understand and experience how real love removes the barriers of age, gender, race and belief.
Maybe a story I heard recently would say it better:

Once upon a time, a wise and learned teacher went to a deserted field with some of his most perceptive students. Together they spent hours talking about life and all it's mysteries. Day passed and they talked through the dark of night.

Hours into the blackness one of the students broke a long silence by asking, "When will we know that night has ended and day has begun?"

One student gazed into the darkness and said, " We will know that night has ended and day has begun when it becomes light enough for us to look at the animals grazing in the field beyond and recognize the difference between the sheep and the goats."

After further silence another student said, "We will know that night has ended and day has begun when it becomes light enough for us to look into the field beyond and recognize the difference between the fig leaves and the grape vines."

After still further silence, the students turned to their teacher and said, "Wise Teacher, you who have taught us so much about life, tell us. When will we know that night has ended and day has begun?"

Looking fondly on them, the Wise Teacher began with slow and deliberate gentleness. "My dear Students," he said, "when it is light enough for you to look into the face of whomever you see and recognize in it your brother or sister, you will know that night has ended and day has begun."

ALSO FROM *ST. JOHN'S PUBLISHING...*

• • •

Parenting a Business, by Donna L. Montgomery, looks at business relationships from a parenting standpoint.

Surviving Motherhood, by Donna L. Montgomery. A look at family relationships written by a mother of eight who is a survivor of motherhood herself.

Kids+ Modeling= Money, by Donna L. Montgomery, is all you need to help your child begin a rewarding and prosperous modeling career. Discover the secrets of modeling success.

• • •

ST. JOHN'S PUBLISHING
6824 OAKLAWN AVENUE
EDINA, MN 55435

Please send me _____ copy (copies) of **Parenting a Business** (ISBN 0-938577-04-2).I am enclosing $14.95 and $1.50 for shipping for each copy.

Please send me _____ copy (copies) of **Surviving Motherhood,** (ISBN 0-938577-00-X). I am enclosing $6.95 and $1.50 for shipping for each copy.

Please send me _____ copy (copies) of **Kids+ Modeling= Money,** (ISBN 0-13-515172-4).I am enclosing $9.95 (hardcover) and $1.50 for shipping for each copy.

NAME _____

ADDRESS _____

_____

_____